Amelia Earhart

Amelia Earhart

Beyond the Grave

W.C. Jameson

TAYLOR TRADE PUBLISHING
Lanham • Boulder • New York • London

Published by Taylor Trade Publishing
An imprint of The Rowman & Littlefield Publishing Group, Inc.
4501 Forbes Boulevard, Suite 200, Lanham, Maryland 20706
www.rowman.com

Unit A, Whitacre Mews, 26-34 Stannary Street, London SE11 4AB, United Kingdom

Distributed by NATIONAL BOOK NETWORK

British Library Cataloguing in Publication Information Available

Library of Congress Cataloging-in-Publication Data
Names: Jameson, W.C., 1942– author.
Title: Amelia Earhart : beyond the grave / W.C. Jameson.
Description: Lanham : Taylor Trade Publishing, [2016] | Series: Beyond the
  grave | Includes bibliographical references.
Identifiers: LCCN 2015037089 | ISBN 9781589799905 (hardback) |
  ISBN 9781589799912 (electronic)
Subjects: LCSH: Earhart, Amelia, 1897–1937. | Women air pilots—
  United States—Biography. | Air pilots—United States—Biography. |
  BISAC: BIOGRAPHY & AUTOBIOGRAPHY / Adventurers &
  Explorers. | BIOGRAPHY & AUTOBIOGRAPHY / Historical. |
  BIOGRAPHY & AUTOBIOGRAPHY / Women.
Classification: LCC TL540.E3 J36 2016 | DDC 629.13092—dc23
LC record available at http://lccn.loc.gov/2015037089

Printed in the United States of America

Contents

Foreword

$\mathcal{T}$o this day, the mysterious disappearance of Amelia M. Earhart during her around-the-world flight in 1937 evokes debate whether her flight was a tragic accident or the result of a covert mission disguised as a goodwill publicity flight that ended unexpectedly without a contingency plan. W.C. Jameson has captured the essence of the latter perspective through the abundance of credible evidence that strongly suggests Amelia Earhart survived a presumed emergency or crash landing in the South Pacific and was taken prisoner. The controversy that arises from this evidence is the fact that, although presumed dead, Amelia was actually repatriated to the United States under a different identity and lived a solitary life while maintaining one of the greatest secrets in aviation history.

In aircraft accident investigation, the investigator must rely on the facts, conditions, and circumstances that are developed from various sources, including the aircraft wreckage, witness information, documents, testimonials, and other credible information to determine the causes and contributing factors of the accident. *Amelia Earhart: Beyond the Grave* is a compelling discussion of fact-based evidence that presents the reader with a logical explanation for why there has never been any wreckage found from Amelia's "specially equipped" Lockheed L-10E Electra or why the U.S. government still classifies numerous documents related to the publicity flight as "top secret."

As an aircraft accident investigator, I have found it easy to dismiss opinions, "pet theories," and good story lines that are not supported by credible evidence. However, W.C. Jameson's presentation of factual information, corroborating evidence from others investigating this flight, and the comparisons and parallels he draws from other historical people and events captured my attention throughout the book. This is a must-read book for those who want to learn about the more intriguing aspects of aviation's greatest mystery flight!

Gregory A. Feith
Former "Go-Team" Captain and Senior Air Safety Investigator
U.S. National Transportation Safety Board (NTSB)

· 1 ·

Woman of Mystery,
Woman of Contradictions

$\mathcal{T}$he Amelia Earhart of popular perception—"The First Lady of the Sky" and "America's Darling"—was quite unlike the private Amelia Earhart. The public Earhart was, in fact, a product of marketing and media, all brilliantly designed, constructed, and masterfully steered by her husband, the publishing and publicity magnate George Palmer Putnam.

The truth is, at the time, Earhart was only one of a number of female aviatrices who gained notice during the early 1900s. Though she was often billed as one of the world's greatest pilots, this was far from true. Earhart possessed a set of skills and accomplishments related to flying and was fearless, to be sure, but not necessarily any more so than a number of other female pilots of the time. She was no better or worse than the rest, but as a result of fearlessness and a desire to break down certain social barriers along with a clever publicity and marketing campaign, she managed better breaks than her contemporaries. She was, without doubt, the most famous.

The private Amelia Earhart was an altogether different person. She was a woman who had a passion for flying, who accomplished a number of impressive deeds, and who turned out to be very lucky.

Earhart was a woman around whom an international mystery eventually swirled, one that had its genesis in 1937 with her reported disappearance, one that continues to intrigue us to this day. It is a grand mystery that is accompanied by a number of correlative mysteries, all of which have generated considerable controversy over what actually happened to the aviatrix, as well as who was involved. The mysteries extended to manipulations orchestrated by the U.S. government and the extent to which international relationships and politics were inserted.

What may be an even greater mystery surrounds the notion that Earhart, following her disappearance, had been held captive by the Japanese for eight years, rescued at the end of the war, and, with governmental assistance, re-patriated to the United States, where she lived out her life under an alias in what amounted to an early-day witness protection program.

More than three-quarters of a century following Earhart's "disappear-ance" during her much ballyhooed around-the-world flight, the questions related to what actually happened to her are still being asked, and the answers continue to be debated. Today, there is an overabundance of Amelia Earhart research and inquiry forums on the Internet that remains active and ongoing.

Any tempting research project demands an extensive literature search prior to undertaking a sophisticated investigation. In the case of Amelia Earhart, it was discovered that there exists an active cadre of Earhart afi-cionados, a large percentage of them aburst with enthusiasm, energy, and commitment but for the most part unskilled at both research and writing. Furthermore, there appears to be little agreement among them relative to what ultimately became of Earhart and her copilot Fred Noonan once they lost radio contact during her famous around-the-world flight. After reading and studying dozens of books and hundreds of articles and Internet sites, as well as interviewing a number of people intimate with flying and with Earhart, it is apparent that there exists a plethora of theories relative to what might have happened to her.

Because of the strong differences of opinion and obvious passion for the subject that can be found among many of the enthusiasts, a degree of hostil-ity exists among some members of the cadre, with occasional sniping at one another throughout the pages of the published books and the Internet post-ings. It leaves the appearance of aggressive competition, insecure egos, and not much cooperation.

Research has been further hampered by the fact that far too many of the available books about Earhart are self-published and vanity press offerings, all of them suffering from the usual and expected lack of competent editing, design, fact checking, and other furbelows one expects with a serious and professional publication about an important topic. A number of these publi-cations have incompletely prepared indexes or none at all, further frustrating interested readers and researchers.

In the end, it became clear that a great deal of work still needed to be undertaken relative to Amelia Earhart—who she was, what she did, her final mission, and what might have become of her.

In the following pages is presented an array of facts and theories relative to the so-called disappearance of Amelia Earhart, evidence related to what befell her, what might have become of her in the years immediately following what the U.S. government claimed was her crash into the ocean and subsequent sinking, and her eventual repatriation to her homeland, where she may have lived for another several decades under an assumed name.

Layered over the mystery of Amelia Earhart's disappearance are a number of others that involve prominent political and military figures who weave in and out of the events that began months prior to Earhart's famous around-the-world flight, mysteries that suggest military conspiracy, political manipulations, cover-up, and outright lying to the American public.

The fact is, the official government position on the fate of Amelia Earhart is a lie. It is hoped that the details relative to a quest for the truth that are presented in this book will contribute to a greater understanding of what happened to America's first lady of the air.

· 2 ·

Origins

$\mathcal{T}$hroughout much of Amelia Earhart's life she pursued a number of career choices, seldom remaining long in any of them. The one thing upon which she maintained a deep and vibrant focus, however, was flying. Flying would eventually define her, it would bring her unheard-of fame, and in time it would lead to her famous disappearance, one of the greatest mysteries in the history of the United States.

On July 24, 1897, Amelia Mary Earhart was born to Amy and Edwin Earhart. The birth took place at the home of Amy's parents in Atchison, Kansas, fifty miles northwest of Kansas City. She was nicknamed "Millie." When Earhart was born, there were only forty-five states, and the principal personal mode of transportation was horse and buggy. Two and one-half years later a sister, Muriel, was born.

The marriage of Amy and Edwin was stormy. Though Edwin held down a job as a claims attorney for a railroad company, his income was somewhat meager. Amy, on the other hand, was used to a higher standard of living. Her father was Judge Alfred Otis, and the Otis family lived in relative luxury. The problem of not having enough money generated strife sufficient to ship Amelia and Muriel to the Otis home, where they were, for the most part, raised and educated. The sisters were enrolled in a private school in Kansas City.

From time to time, Amelia and Muriel would return to the home of their parents, but peace and harmony were in short supply. In addition to the problems associated with having too little money, Edwin had taken to drinking. Instability reigned, further abetted by the fact that Edwin was transferred often as a result of his job. In time he was fired, and the family

4

income fell to nothing. In 1915, Amy and Edwin separated. Edwin's alcoholism was to have a profound effect on Amelia, one that surfaced often during subsequent years.

Amelia eventually graduated from Chicago's Hyde Park High School in June 1916, the sixth such school she attended in four years. By this time, she was known for her competence seasoned with a streak of independence.

Around the time Amelia graduated from high school, mother Amy received an inheritance that provided for a good living, and in time, she and Edwin were reunited and the family was living in Kansas City. In the fall of 1916, Amelia enrolled at Ogontz College in Rydal, Pennsylvania. Ogontz began in 1850 as the Chestnut Street Female Academy in Philadelphia. In 1883 it moved to the Elkin Park estate of financier Jay Cooke and was renamed Ogontz after a Sandusky Indian chief. In 1916, the institution moved to Rydal in the suburban Abington Township. Today, Ogontz is part of the Pennsylvania State University System.

It was while at Ogontz that Amelia began taking notice of women who excelled in positions normally dominated by males, women who were becoming doctors, lawyers, and bank presidents and running for political office.

During the Christmas holiday of 1917, Amelia traveled to Toronto, Canada, to visit sister Muriel, who was living there. It was in Toronto that Amelia first observed soldiers who had returned from World War I, many of whom were wounded and maimed. This impressed her deeply, and with a keen sense of commitment she undertook a Red Cross–sponsored course that would yield a qualification as a nurse's aide. When Amelia completed the requirements, she began serving at Toronto's Spadina Military Hospital.

For the most part, Amelia was involved in the menial yet important tasks of emptying bedpans, making beds, working in the kitchen, serving food, and washing patients. Caring for the war-wounded had a deep impact on the young woman, and she never forgot the experience.

While she was serving at the hospital, Amelia met a man who was an officer in the Royal Flying Corps. One day, he invited her to accompany him to an airfield outside of Toronto to watch planes taking off and landing. In her book *20 Hrs. 40 Min.: Our Flight in the Friendship*, Amelia wrote that it was this experience that generated her "first urge to fly."

The war had finally wound down, and Amelia returned to the United States in 1919. While her head was filled with thoughts of airplanes and flying, she enrolled in a premedical program at Columbia University in New York City. After completing one year at the university, Amelia decided to join her parents, who by this time were living in Los Angeles, California. She arrived during the summer of 1920. While in Los Angeles, Amelia and father Edwin attended an air show at Long Beach's Daugherty Field. Here, she confessed to him that she had always wanted to fly. In response, Edwin made arrangements for his daughter to be taken up in an airplane.

The following day after Edwin paid the ten-dollar fee, Amelia experienced flight for the first time. Before the plane landed, she made a commitment to herself that she was going to learn to pilot an aircraft. She began making plans to take lessons, and she was determined to receive them from a female pilot she had read about.

The pilot was Nita Snook, and she had an immediate and deep effect on Earhart. Snook agreed to take the young woman on as a student. To pay for her lessons, Amelia offered Snook some of the Liberty Bonds she possessed. Snook agreed they were sufficient to get far enough along in the lessons to make a determination whether or not her new student had any competencies as a flyer. Earhart took her first lesson on the morning of January 3, 1921, in a Kinner airplane, built by the Kinner Airplane and Motor Corporation.

Most of Earhart's time was now spent at the airfield absorbing the lessons provided by Snook, as well as in conversations with Bert Kinner, who designed the aircraft. In turn, both Snook and Kinner were impressed with their new student. After soloing, Earhart asked for and received instruction in flying-related emergencies. She practiced these for hours, according to some, and soon achieved the skill of her instructor. Somehow, in 1921 Earhart saved enough money from her job at a telephone company to purchase her own airplane, a Kinner Airster. What income she had remaining after paying her living expenses funded her weekend flying.

With her passion for flying dominating her activities, as well as her need to hold down a full time job, Amelia had little time for a social life. The few men she met were usually encountered at the air shows she attended with Snook. She had little time for the young men who, to her, seemed unfocused and irresponsible, and she was more taken with older ones. In time, Amelia was attending concerts and other outings with a man named Samuel Chapman, originally from Massachusetts and a graduate of Tufts University. Chapman, in fact, was renting a room at the home of Earhart's parents. In time, the two became quite close.

During late 1921, Amelia entered the Air Rodeo held at the Sierra Airdome in Pasadena, California. She, along with another female pilot named Aloyfia McLintic, were the featured flyers. Amelia made the decision to attempt a new altitude record for women. She accomplished this by ascending more than fourteen thousand feet.

Though Amelia was garnering some publicity as an accomplished aviatrix, she earned no money at it. In fact, she was comfortable in the notion that what she was doing was a sport, and the idea of making a living at it was foreign to her.

On May 16, 1923, Amelia was granted certificate number 6017 by the Fédération Aéronautique Internationale. The certificate stated that she was certified as an "Aviator Pilot." Of the thousands of such certificates that had been issued over the years, Earhart's was one of only about twenty issued to women. Interestingly, on her application Earhart listed her birthdate as July 24, 1898, making her one year younger than she was, a deception she was to maintain for the rest of her life.

In 1924, Amy and Edwin's oft-contentious marriage finally ended, and they were granted a divorce. Amy decided she wanted to move from Los Angeles to Boston, where daughter Muriel was attending college. Amy told Amelia that she would pay her tuition if she would return to Columbia and pursue her college education. Amy paid off the note on Earhart's airplane, and a short time later it was sold. With the money from the sale, Earhart purchased a Kinner automobile and drove her mother from Los Angeles to Boston. She then enrolled for the fall 1924 semester at Columbia University.

During the spring of 1925, Amy suffered some financial setbacks as a result of the deteriorating economy. Amelia left school and traveled to Medford, Massachusetts, to find a job. Once ensconced in her new residence, she joined the Boston chapter of the National Aeronautic Association. Bert Kinner learned of Earhart's connection with a new airport near Quincy and offered her a plane to exhibit. In between demonstrations, said Kinner, she was free to fly the craft as much as she wished.

Samuel Chapman was apparently more enamored of Earhart than she was of him. He arrived in Massachusetts a few weeks after she did and landed a job at the Boston Edison Company. The two renewed their friendship, and a short time later Chapman proposed marriage. Not completely understanding Earhart's streak of independence, he explained to her that he would not tolerate a wife working outside the home. She turned him down. The two remained friends and continued dating, but it never went beyond that. As time passed, Amelia moved in and out of other jobs, including teaching foreign students in a university extension program and being a social worker.

On May 21, 1927, Charles A. Lindbergh completed a nonstop solo flight from New York to Paris. Overnight he became a national hero and was celebrated throughout the world. Earhart read the newspaper accounts of the flight and the intrepid flyer with interest, excitement, and fascination.

The following year Earhart turned thirty. She had grown into a woman of numerous competencies and accomplishments and held a passion not only for flying but also for adventure. She was confident that her flying abilities and her dreams could propel her to the heights reached by Lindbergh. The international stage was being set for her grand entrance.

· 3 ·

Enter George Palmer Putnam

In 1928, Amelia Earhart was employed as a social worker at the Denison House, a settlement residence in Boston. Denison House was a focal point for immigrants. Here, they were provided instruction in the English language, nursing, dancing, and other topics. Relief programs were established as well as activities for the children and clubs for the adults. Earhart, who served as a teacher and helped generate publicity for the organization, was paid sixty dollars per month.

In April of that year, Earhart received a telephone call from Hilton H. Railey. Railey explained he was calling on behalf of New York publisher George Palmer Putnam and wanted to discuss the possibilities of her involvement in a flight that carried some amount of risk but offered incredible rewards. Amelia agreed to meet with Railey a few hours later to discuss his proposition.

Railey explained to Earhart that Admiral Richard E. Byrd's plane, a trimotor Fokker, was undergoing an intense mechanical examination and upgrade in Boston in preparation for a flight across the Atlantic. Byrd was a pioneering American aviator and noted polar explorer. The sponsors of the adventure desired to have an American woman involved in the project. During the early phases of planning for the flight, a Mrs. Frederick Guest was to be the female aviatrix. In fact, Guest, a wealthy native of London, had purchased the Fokker trimotor for the adventure. In the end, however, Guest decided it would be more appropriate for a younger woman to take her place.

The task of identifying and locating the appropriate female pilot to be involved in this adventure fell to George Palmer Putnam of the publishing house of G. P. Putnam and Sons. The publishing company had plans to commission an author to write a book about the landmark flight. At the time, Amelia Earhart had garnered an impressive level of visibility as a result of her flying accomplishments, one of a number of women involved in flying at the time. In addition, she was attractive, well spoken, and poised. She was, in short, a publicist's dream.

Earhart expressed her interest, and ten days later she found herself being subjected to an interview with the flight's sponsors at the offices of G. P. Putnam and Sons Publishing Company in New York City. Here she was introduced to George Palmer Putnam. The interview, as well as the beginning of her relationship with Putnam, was to forever change Earhart's path as well as the image of women throughout the world. It was also a catalyst that would lead to one of the greatest mysteries in history.

George Palmer Putnam II was born on September 7, 1887, in Rye, New York, a suburb of New York City near Long Island Sound. He was the grandson of and named after the publishing tycoon. Most people referred to George II as "G. P."

Knowing that his older brother, Robert, would eventually assume control of the publishing business, Putnam decided to seek his fortune and his adventure elsewhere. With little money, he traveled to Bend, Oregon, where he found some satisfaction. There, he married Dorothy Binney, a native of Connecticut, and before long a son, David, was born. Putnam prospered as a businessman and publisher and was even elected mayor of Bend. In 1914, he was named secretary to Oregon's governor Withycombe.

In 1916, Putnam's father passed away. According to plans, brother Robert took over the publishing house. By this time, the United States had become heavily involved in World War I. In December 1918, Putnam enlisted in the army and was soon commissioned as an artillery officer. Not long afterward, Robert Putnam died as a result of the flu epidemic that swept the Eastern Seaboard, and G. P. returned to New York to become involved in the management of the publishing company. In large part because of his energy, enthusiasm, and keen business sense, the publishing house prospered over the next decade. During this time, Putnam honed the marketing and publicizing skills that were to serve him well for the rest of his life.

George Palmer Putnam II was also vitally interested in the movie business. He convinced film producer Jesse Lansky to back the making of Hollywood's first aviation movie, *Wings*, starring Clara Bow, Gary Cooper, and Buddy Rogers. It was also the first film to win an Academy Award. In addition, Putnam was instrumental in the publication of the book *We*, by

Charles A. Lindbergh. It was a best seller and earned the publishing company a lot of money. With this particular success under his belt, Putnam was on the lookout for the next aviation best seller when he learned about Amelia Earhart.

Everyone present at the interview at the publishing house came away impressed with Earhart and lost no time in discussing a potential contract. After Earhart thanked everyone and was preparing to leave the office, Putnam offered to escort her to the train station. A few days after returning to Boston, Earhart received a phone call informing her that she had been accepted as part of the crew that would conduct the flight across the Atlantic.

It was immediately arranged for Earhart to meet the pilot, Wilmer L. Stultz, and the mechanic, Louis E. Gordon. She got along well with both men and eagerly anticipated the forthcoming adventure. She learned, however, that she was only to be a passenger and that she would not be handling any of the airplane's controls. In the time leading up to the flight, Earhart studied books on navigation and nautical astronomy.

While preparations were being made, Putnam, accompanied by his wife, Dorothy, made several trips to Boston to meet with Earhart. The couple invited her out to dinner, concerts, and social gatherings and introduced her to famous and prominent people.

Byrd's Fokker trimotor seaplane was named *Friendship*, and the crossing was tagged "The Friendship Flight." With Stultz, Gordon, and Earhart aboard, it lifted off from Boston Harbor near dawn on Sunday morning, June 3, 1928. The first stop was at Trepassey, Newfoundland, to refuel in preparation for the oceanic crossing. On arriving, however, weather conditions took a turn for the worse, and the scheduled takeoff for Europe was delayed for thirteen days.

While detained at Trepassey, Earhart discovered Stultz had a serious drinking problem. Already nervous and cautious because of her father's difficulties with drink, Earhart began to have concerns about Stultz's abilities to pilot the trimotor across the Atlantic.

Back home, Putnam was working overtime sending out press releases to the country's newspapers with the story of the first woman to fly across the Atlantic. Photographs of the tall, slim, and attractive Earhart captivated the attention of readers, and she was being referred to by the publicity-minded Putnam as "Lady Lindy."

On Sunday, June 17, the weather finally broke and was deemed suitable for takeoff. The seaplane lifted off at 11:00 a.m. bound for Europe. Twenty hours and forty minutes later, the plane landed at Burry Port, Wales. The crossing set a record, and Earhart went down in the history books as the first woman to have flown across the Atlantic Ocean. Though she never once assisted in flying the aircraft and was little more than a passenger, her life had been completely altered. Most of the publicity centered on her. From this day on, Amelia Earhart would forevermore be a celebrity.

· 4 ·

Celebrity

$\mathcal{A}$melia Earhart was stunned to discover that, on her arrival in Europe, she was regarded as a celebrity. Disembarking from the *Friendship* with nothing but the clothes she was wearing and a small pack that contained little more than a comb and a toothbrush, she was pulled into a whirlwind of activity. Within the next few days, she would be feted, participate in a parade, meet Lady Nancy Astor and department store magnate H. Gordon Selfridge, sign a book contract, purchase an airplane, and be gifted several trunks filled with fine, expensive clothes. As a result of Putnam's publicity campaign, Earhart had become the center of attention.

Throughout all of the notice and recognition she was receiving, Earhart was constantly trying to point out that all of the credit for the successful flight was due to Stultz and Gordon. The press, however, was interested only in Earhart, and the articles featured extensive portraits of her, often to the complete omission of the pilot and mechanic. Earhart's charm, good looks, and charisma steamrolled the reporters to the point of obsession.

Ten days after landing in Wales, Earhart, Stultz, and Gordon were in Southampton, England, preparing to board the SS *President Roosevelt* for the return trip to New York. Stultz remained drunk throughout most of the cruise and locked himself in his cabin. Earhart attempted to talk with him, but he resisted her efforts. She decided she would never work with Bill Stultz again.

The ship arrived at New York Harbor on July 6. Waiting there to greet the successful Atlantic trio was New York mayor Jimmy Walker in his own yacht. The *Friendship* crew boarded the vessel and was greeted by the mayor, George Palmer Putnam, and assorted dignitaries. Following this was a ticker-tape parade down Broadway and a series of receptions that lasted well into the next morning. G. P. Putnam appeared to have orchestrated most of the celebrations. In Earhart, he saw the value of her contrived and publicized accomplishment and the attendant fame, all seasoned with a charming and magnetic personality. It is clear that by this time Putnam viewed Earhart from several different perspectives, and one of them was related to the notion that she was highly marketable. Publisher and publicist Putnam had visions of even greater fame for Earhart coupled with more money and prestige.

Putnam arranged a tour for Earhart, Stultz, and Gordon that went from New York to Boston and then on to Chicago. Earhart was prominently displayed before huge audiences, always in the forefront of the pilot and mechanic. When reporters asked questions, they addressed only Earhart. When the tour was completed, Earhart locked herself away for a time to work on the book she would title *20 Hrs. 40 Min.: Our Flight in the Friendship*, the story of her trip across the Atlantic Ocean. When she finally came up for air and examined her accumulated mail, Earhart found she had received dozens of invitations for public appearances and lectures. Putnam kept her name in the newspapers, often accompanied by a photograph of her alongside some dignitary or celebrity.

Another major recognition had been bestowed on Earhart following the transatlantic flight. She was awarded the Distinguished Flying Cross, the first woman to receive that honor. The DFC is traditionally awarded to any officer or enlisted member of the armed forces who is distinguished as a result of heroism or extraordinary achievement while participating in aerial flight. In 1929, Congress passed special legislation that allowed the award to be presented to Orville and Wilbur Wright. Since then, in addition to Amelia Earhart, other civilians who have won that award include Wiley Post, Jacqueline Cochran, Eugene Ely, and Roscoe Turner. By September, Earhart had finished her book and decided it was time to start flying again.

The first thing Earhart did was to make a solo flight cross-country to California in her new airplane, an Avro Avian she had purchased from Lady Heath. It was the first Atlantic-to-Pacific coast flight ever by a woman. While in California, she attended the National Air Races. When she returned to New York on October 16, she went straight to work as a member of the *Cosmopolitan* magazine editorial staff.

On March 29, 1929, Earhart passed the tests for a transport pilot license from the Department of Commerce. She was now certified as a transport pilot, one of only seven women to have earned the ranking.

During the summer of 1929, Earhart was hired by Transcontinental Air Transport to use her celebrity to lobby for the notion that flying was safe for women. TAT, which would evolve into Trans World Airlines, had just opened up air service from New York to Los Angeles and was soliciting customers. On July 7, the first flight lifted off from New York. Earhart was among the passengers. The plane made a fuel stop in Phoenix, where it was greeted by Charles Lindbergh and his wife, Anne. The Lindberghs flew the rest of the way to Los Angeles in the company of the aviatrix.

Earhart eventually traded in her Avro Avian for a Lockheed Vega. The single-pilot plane boasted a nine-cylinder Pratt and Whitney engine. Earhart entered her aircraft in the first all-female air race at Clover Field in Santa Monica, California. Nineteen of the most well-known women pilots in America were entered. They took off on August 18 bound for Cleveland, Ohio. Earhart came in third.

At Cleveland, a meeting was held for the purpose of establishing an association of licensed women pilots. Invitations had been sent to 120 certified aviatrices, and ninety-nine showed up. Earhart was elected first president of the group, which named itself the Ninety-Nines.

On November 22, 1929, Earhart was in Los Angeles with her Lockheed Vega to attempt a new women's speed record. Her average speed was 184.17 mph. The principal purpose of the trip as designed by George Putnam, however, was to keep her face and activities in the news and in front of the public.

Earhart went on to set three world speed records in her Lockheed Vega on June 25 and July 5, 1930. Around this time, air travel was a young yet growing enterprise, and Earhart found herself in the middle of it. She partnered with Paul Collins and Eugene Vidal to establish a new airline. Collins and Vidal had been involved with the development of Transcontinental Air Transport. Earhart was to be vice president of public relations and was primarily associated with the promotion of an hourly shuttle connecting New York, Philadelphia, and Washington, D.C. On September 1, 1930, New York, Philadelphia, and Washington Airways opened for business. In a short time, NYPWA was renamed as the more manageable Ludington Line. Charles and Nicholas Ludington were the primary financial backers for the line. With her executive responsibilities with TAT, the Ludington Line, and her schedule of paid lectures and personal appearances, Earhart was traveling most of every week. She was also becoming one of the most recognizable and prominent women not only in the United States but in the world.

· 5 ·

Marriage

$\mathcal{G}$eorge Palmer Putnam II remained busy booking appearances for Earhart as well as making certain that her activities and accomplishments were being reported in the nation's major newspapers. In 1930, Putnam's uncle passed away, leaving his interest in G. P. Putnam's Sons Publishing Company to his son, Palmer C. Putnam. George II had been with the company for ten years. For several weeks, Palmer and George discussed the publishing business in general and the future of the family publishing company in particular. In the end, George sold Palmer his interest in the business. Some money exchanged hands. In addition, Palmer presented George with a promissory note for $100,000. George immediately went to work for another New York publishing company—Brewer and Warren.

While Putnam was busy promoting Earhart and spending much of his time with her in Los Angeles, his wife, Dorothy, was in Las Vegas filing for divorce. At the time, many were convinced Putnam had eyes only for Earhart and that it became quite obvious to his wife. The divorce was granted on December 19, 1929. Earhart and Putnam were married on February 7, 1931. She was thirty-three years old; he was forty-three. Many have argued that the marriage for these two intense, career-minded individuals was one of convenience and profit. Others have maintained the position that the two were, in fact, deeply in love and quite devoted to each other. Putnam was an adept manager and coordinator of publicity, both of which were vital to Earhart's expanding career. And for Putnam, Earhart was a valuable commodity, one that had the potential for many years of cash flow from books and personal appearances. It was said that the two made an agreement that if one or the other decided that their individual careers were not progressing as a result of the marriage, they would have it dissolved. Following the wedding, both

Earhart and Putnam were so busy with their careers that they had little opportunity for a honeymoon. The newlyweds settled in at Putnam's home in Rye, New York.

Author Vincent Loomis wrote that Earhart's friends were convinced Putnam was not in love with Amelia nor she with him. The arrangement, says Loomis, "was one that cemented their future partnership in aviation. She wanted to fly; he wanted to promote her as the best flyer in the world." Putnam's greatest skill was as a promoter, and with Earhart he saw a huge payoff. Putnam was also regarded by many as a master manipulator, and in truth he was proved to be such when he assumed responsibility for Earhart's career.

The fact is, despite all of the publicity and exposure, Amelia Earhart was an average pilot, no better or worse than a handful of other female aviatrices during that period. In head-to-head flying competitions, Earhart rarely won and at times placed last. Earhart, however, had several things going for her relative to her climb toward celebrity: she was attractive, she had a sense of style (women began to dress like her), she was an excellent writer, she had poise and charm, she was fearless, and most of all, she was married to an experienced and polished publicist. The public Amelia Earhart, in the end, was a product of marketing and publicity.

Shortly after her marriage, Earhart was introduced to a new kind of aircraft—the autogyro, a forerunner to the helicopter. The manufacturer of the autogyro employed Earhart to demonstrate the new invention. Following a relatively short instruction period, Earhart took off in the autogyro and climbed to 18,415 feet, a record height. Numerous headlines were generated by Putnam and filed across the country and the world relative to this accomplishment. Between May 29 and June 6, 1931, Earhart flew an autogyro from Newark, New Jersey, to Oakland, California, becoming the first woman to do so. Press releases followed.

So busy was Earhart that she was rarely seen with Putnam. Little time passed before she was once again in the nation's headlines, this time with new plans to fly solo across the Atlantic Ocean in her Lockheed Vega. Prior to the flight, Earhart steeped herself in learning how to pilot via instruments. Heretofore, Earhart flew using only maps and by sophisticated guesswork, the so-called seat-of-the-pants flying technique.

On May 20, 1932, Earhart took off from Harbor Grace, Newfoundland. Thirteen hours and thirty minutes later, she landed at Londonderry in Northern Ireland, the first woman to have flown solo across the Atlantic Ocean. Following her amazing performance was an extended tour of Europe, where she was feted almost daily. She was received by royalty and by the pope. During the tour, she was joined by Putnam. At one point, Earhart and Putnam found themselves in the company of Archbishop Pacelli, who later became Pope Pius XII, and a priest named James Francis Kelley. Though no one could have known at the time, Father Kelley would reappear thirteen years later to play an important role in Amelia Earhart's life.

When Earhart and her husband returned to New York, she was lauded as the "first lady of the air." One newspaper proclaimed her the best-known woman in the world. Parades followed, and soon she was inundated with more invitations for public appearances. Life was busy for Amelia Earhart.

A short time following her Newfoundland-to-Ireland flight, Earhart received a telegram of congratulations from Eleanor Roosevelt, the wife of presidential candidate Franklin D. Roosevelt, who, at the time, was the governor of New York. George Putnam soon resigned from Brewer and Warren and was shortly thereafter named the head of the editorial board for Paramount, the motion picture company. He maintained offices in New York and Hollywood in order to keep up with his new enterprises. When time permitted, Earhart would often join him at the studios. In August 1932, she flew the Lockheed to Los Angeles. On the return trip, she left Los Angeles on August 24 and flew nonstop to Newark, New Jersey, in nine hours and five minutes. The distance of 2,447 miles without refueling was a new women's record.

Late in 1932, Earhart and husband Putnam were invited to dine with Franklin D. and Eleanor Roosevelt at their Hyde Park estate. The four soon became close friends. Earhart and Putnam were invited to Roosevelt's inauguration following his election to the presidency.

Little did Earhart realize that Roosevelt and his staff would soon impress upon her the need for her participation in a mission vital to the nation's welfare. During the 1930s, according to author David K. Bowman, Roosevelt often asked "wealthy and well-connected friends and amateurs to accept intelligence assignments while on their travels." During the impending war with Japan, the United States was in desperate need of intelligence.

· 6 ·

Hawaii to California

$\mathcal{B}$y the end of 1932, Amelia Earhart was thirty-five years of age with a long list of impressive accomplishments. She continued to tour the country lecturing to sold-out venues. Though the Ludington Line went out of business, a short time later the principals Earhart, Collins, and Vidal, along with an investor named Sam Solomon, developed yet another airline. It was initially named National Airways but soon came to be called Boston-Maine Airways. Earhart was named vice president. During the incorporation, Vidal was named director of the Bureau of Air Commerce in Washington, D.C. In time, Boston-Maine Airways grew to be part of the Delta Air Lines system.

As president of the United States, Franklin D. Roosevelt sponsored a number of new airports and airways facilities. He also saw the need for a more sophisticated radiotelegraph communications and navigation system. In addition, Roosevelt was also instrumental in establishing strategically placed airports and landing strips, along with communications facilities, throughout much of the world where the United States had interests.

In 1933, a cadre of Hawaiian businessmen sponsored a flight from Hawaii to the West Coast of the United States, offering a prize of $10,000. Earhart professed interest. It would be another challenge, another payday, and another opportunity to remain in the public eye.

In 1934, Earhart hired Paul Mantz as her technical adviser. His job was to prepare her Vega for the flight from Hawaii to California. Mantz came with a hefty set of credentials: he owned United Air Services, he had an excellent pilot rating in the army (though he had been discharged for not following orders), and he was a stunt pilot for motion pictures. Like Earhart, Mantz owned and flew a Lockheed Vega.

Recent flying regulations required any aircraft crossing oceans to have a radio transmitter powerful enough to maintain continuous communication. For the Vega, Earhart required a two-channel, 3,105-kilocycle radio for airway and nighttime communications and 6,210 kilocycles for long-range daytime transmissions. The 6,210-kilocycle transmitter had a longer range. Such systems required an effective antenna. For the Vega, Mantz installed a state-of-the-art trailing wire antenna that could be reeled in and out much like a fishing line.

During the Christmas holidays of 1934, Earhart, along with Mantz and his wife, took a liner to Hawaii. Her Vega was strapped to the tennis deck of the ship and offloaded onto a barge for transportation to Fleet Air Base in Pearl Harbor. From here it was flown to Wheeler Field for a final checkup before undertaking the transpacific flight.

At 4:44 p.m. Hawaiian Standard Time on January 11, 1935, Earhart took off from Wheeler Field. One hour later, she reeled out the trailing wire antenna and broadcast her first message on 3,105 kilocycles. Putnam was listening to the transmission in Honolulu and responded that her signal had less volume than it should have and was difficult to understand. Throughout the flight, Earhart transmitted on both 3,105 and 6,210 kilocycles with mixed results but was by and large pleased with the system. Radio communication difficulties were to plague Earhart in the future.

Eighteen hours and seventeen minutes later, Earhart landed at Oakland. A crowd estimated to number five thousand was there to welcome her. At the time, Earhart was the only woman to have flown across the Pacific Ocean from Hawaii and the only pilot to accomplish it solo. Once again, she made the front pages. The flight, Earhart knew, would guarantee her a positive image and an enduring position in aviation. With encouragement from Putnam, she was beginning to entertain the notion of one of the greatest adventures ever—an around-the-world flight.

More flights followed, more praises heaped upon her. Putnam set about the task of raising money to purchase a newer and better aircraft, one that could make an around-the-world voyage.

In the meantime, Putnam's cousin, Palmer, was forced to declare bankruptcy, one of the results being that he still owed G. P. $75,000 that would never be paid. Though still employed by Paramount Pictures, G. P.'s paycheck was insufficient for him to maintain the lifestyle to which he had become accustomed. Furthermore, it certainly would not fund a new airplane for Earhart.

In 1935, after renting out the house in Rye, New York, Putnam and Earhart moved into a small house in Toluca Lake, California, a suburb of North Hollywood. Amelia decided to enter her Vega in the National Air

Races in Cleveland to be held in August. She came in fifth place and won $500. After returning to California, Earhart went into business with Mantz setting up a flight school. G. P. would handle the publicity. Earhart and Mantz were described as a "solid team" and were rarely seen apart.

Trouble was not long in coming. In September, Myrtle Mantz sued her husband for divorce, naming Earhart as the other woman responsible for the breakup. Before the year was out, Mantz and Putnam grew at odds with each other over the way the latter conducted business.

In November, Earhart and Putnam attended a dinner hosted by the president of Purdue University. At the time, Earhart was serving as a part-time counselor for women at the school. During the event, Earhart and Putnam were introduced to a number of the university's benefactors, including the wealthy industrialist David Ross. Putnam explained the need for a new airplane suitable for an around-the-world journey but stated that the aircraft could also serve as a flying laboratory for Purdue's aviation research orientation. Eighty thousand dollars was raised, and within weeks a new twin-engine Lockheed Electra was delivered.

Earhart lost no time in contacting Harry Manning. Earhart first met Manning after her trip across the Atlantic with Stultz and Gordon. Manning was the captain of the SS *Roosevelt*, which carried the crew back to the United States. Later, Manning would be awarded a Congressional Medal of Honor for rescuing the crew of a freighter during a severe Atlantic storm. Manning was also a pilot and was regarded by some as a competent course plotter. Earhart invited Manning to accompany her on the around-the-world flight as her navigator.

Flights around the world had been made previously. In 1924, a U.S. Army Air Service plane made the trip in 175 days. In 1932, a man named Wolfgang von Gronau made it in 110 days in a seaplane. Wiley Post, flying solo in 1933, did it in seven days and eighteen hours. None of these flights, however, crossed the wide expanse of the Pacific Ocean. Furthermore, never had a woman attempted such a feat. In 1936, when time permitted, Earhart and Manning would meet in New York to discuss details of her trip.

One year earlier, Pan American Airways captain Edwin Musick and navigator Fred Noonan surveyed the Pacific Ocean in order to determine the practicality of transoceanic flights. A major problem involved with such an undertaking was the scarcity and incompatibility of communications systems. The two men would eventually make recommendations to facilitate travel across the wide Pacific. Fred Noonan would soon assume a consequential role in Earhart's future.

· 7 ·

Flight around the World: Preparation

$\mathcal{B}$oth Amelia Earhart and G. P. Putnam were riding the high-profile publicity and financial wave of Earhart's accomplishments and popularity during the late 1920s and early 1930s. As a result of the efforts of Putnam, Earhart had her name attached to lines of luggage, suits, pajamas, sports outfits, and stationery.

Putnam worked almost full time keeping Earhart's name and photo-graph in the nation's and the world's newspapers. Now, he realized, was the time for the greatest accomplishment ever for a woman pilot—an around-the-world flight. Though there were a number of skilled and credentialed female pilots in the United States, they had neither the charisma of Amelia Earhart nor the publicity machine in the form of the skilled G. P. Putnam backing them. It was time.

Most of Earhart's aerial activities and accomplishments were widely publicized, but her flying disasters were kept out of the newspapers as much as Putnam could manage it. Once, when taking off at the Abilene, Texas, airport, Earhart crashed her plane. Later, a letter of reprimand was sent to her from the Department of Commerce. At least one newspaper report described Earhart as having been careless and using bad judgment.

On September 17, 1931, Earhart wrecked the Pitcairn autogyro while attempting a landing at Detroit. Earhart was aware that among many flyers—male and female alike—there was not much regard for her ability as a pilot. According to most observers, her flying skills were at best aver-age. Louise Thaden noted that Earhart "was able to follow a manual to the letter, but her flying instincts were not well honed." In order to bolster her image and reputation, Earhart knew she needed to make a significant flying achievement.

Earhart's new airplane was a Lockheed Electra 10E, registration number NR16020. Built to certain specifications, however, this Electra had larger Pratt and Whitney engines, larger fuel tanks, and no cabin windows. Earhart hired Ruckins "Bo" McNeely as a full-time mechanic. McNeely had six years of experience as an overhaul mechanic with Pratt and Whitney. Earhart tested the Electra for the first time on July 21, 1936, and deemed it suitable. Three days later she took possession of it. It was her thirty-ninth birthday.

For further testing and to gain more experience with the new craft, Earhart entered the 1936 New York to Los Angeles Bendix Air Race. With copilot Helen Richey, she finished last in a field of five and received $500 in prize money. Earhart consoled herself about the loss by insisting that the thirty hours of flying time in the new Electra was worth the effort.

For the next several weeks, Earhart studied maps and charts and made preliminary plans for an around-the-world flight. The details for such an undertaking were massive, including licensing in the different countries, passports, visas, landing rights, overflying rights, maintenance, communications, weather, fuel availability, insurance, lodging, finances, and more. Added to this mound of details was the fact that Earhart wanted to fly across the Pacific Ocean. Previous around-the-world flights bypassed this huge body of water by navigating close to the coasts of Canada, Alaska, Japan, China, and Southeast Asia. For Earhart, it would be necessary to stop at one or more locations in the ocean for refueling and maintenance.

In anticipation of the need for future commercial air routes, the Bureau of Air Commerce had established small colonies on some remote Pacific Islands and constructed airfields. In 1936, this responsibility was turned over to the Department of the Interior. One of the locations selected was Howland Island, some 1,900 miles southwest of the Hawaiian Islands. Howland Island was to figure prominently in Earhart's future.

Earhart soon realized she needed assistance with the immense logistics of the flight. She turned to her friend, Eleanor Roosevelt. With the help of the First Lady and her husband, a rather odd decision had been arrived at: the Department of State and the U.S. Navy assumed the responsibilities for most of the arrangements for the around-the-world civilian flight, an adventure that many referred to as a "stunt."

Manning determined that telegraphy would be an utmost necessity for the flight. In order to communicate with coastal stations and ships at sea and for direction finding, it would be essential to transmit on the international standard distress and calling frequency of 500 kilocycles. Celestial navigation would be helpful, but in order to locate a tiny speck such as Howland Island in the middle of the Pacific Ocean would, according to Manning, require more sophisticated instruments.

In November, Earhart went to New York to discuss her communication needs with a representative of the Western Electric Company. Arrangements for transmitting and receiving on 500 kilocycles were made, but such transmissions would require a 250-foot trailing wire antenna. A Bendix radio receiver was installed in the Electra. It was a prototype and had, in fact, just been manufactured but never field-tested. The receiver would accommodate 200 kilocycles through 10,000 kilocycles.

On February 12, 1937, Earhart publicly announced her plans for the around-the-world flight. With Putnam's help, the announcement was carried in newspapers in dozens of countries. With her at the announcement was Harry Manning, whom she introduced as her navigator. On February 17, Earhart, Putnam, Manning, and McNeely set out in the Electra from the Newark airport and headed west. Her first stop was Cleveland, Ohio, and on the following morning they would fly to Burbank, California. Manning was the navigator. At one point, Manning provided a position report to Earhart indicating that they were in Kansas. In truth, however, they were in Oklahoma several miles south of the Kansas border. Putnam began manifesting concerns about Manning's ability to navigate.

In March, Pan American Airways agreed to assist Earhart with her flight. In the meantime, Manning attempted to familiarize himself with the Bendix receiver and experienced difficulties at the outset. When Earhart tried the equipment, it likewise frustrated her. Putnam continued to harbor suspicions related to Manning's navigational abilities and confessed this to Earhart. It was suggested that they allow Manning to navigate them on a flight from Burbank to San Francisco, swing out some distance over the ocean for the return flight, and see whether he could route them back to the point of origin. Employing the newly installed direction-finding apparatus as well as celestial navigation, Manning was off by twenty miles by the time they approached Burbank on the return leg of the trip. Putnam determined that it would be necessary to obtain either a more sophisticated radio direction finder or a more competent navigator.

On returning to Burbank, Putnam made arrangements to meet with a man named Fred Noonan. Noonan had been the chief navigator for Pan American Airways, had recently left the job, and was living in Oakland. Noonan was forty-three years old, had been employed by Pan American for seven years, and was regarded by many as one of the top aerial navigators in the world.

Putnam had suggested to Mantz that he accompany Earhart on the first leg of the flight from Oakland to Honolulu. He agreed. On landing, Mantz would then be responsible for monitoring the servicing for the aircraft. True to his calling, Putnam had arranged for Earhart to have several press conferences in Honolulu. Putnam planned to ask Noonan to accompany Manning to aid in the navigation. Manning, for his part, often expressed the opinion that Earhart lacked sufficient experience with the aircraft for an around-the-world flight. Author Vincent Loomis expressed the opinion that, based on Earhart's history, she was not a good candidate for long-distance flying. He pointed out that she suffered from recurring bouts of illness after long periods of stress and that the tension of a long flight could lead to impaired judgment.

Putnam and Manning met with Noonan. Noonan agreed to travel with them as far as Howland Island. During this portion of the flight, he would have a chance to examine the navigational equipment. Noonan also requested an octant for celestial navigation. The Electra's call letters would be KHAQQ and would transmit on 500, 3,105, or 6,210 kilocycles using both telegraphy and voice during the flight.

· 8 ·

Trouble with Japan

*W*hile Amelia Earhart and a few other female pilots were focusing on their chosen paths and while a small percentage of Americans and Europeans were finding delight in following the adventures of these intrepid women, the rest of the world was in turmoil.

America, as well as much of Europe and elsewhere, was mired in an economic depression. Unemployment was at a record high, and, when it came to the government, the nation's mood was one of disappointment and suspicion. In Europe, Adolf Hitler was making headlines with his rise to power. Spain was involved in a civil war.

What preoccupied the thoughts of many an elected politician, however, was the military buildup in Japan as well as the aggressive attitudes of the leaders of that country. Japan already occupied Korea, had recently invaded Manchuria, and was moving its forces into China. Japan's leaders removed the country from membership in the League of Nations in 1933 and served notice that it would annul its commitment to the arms treaties. Around the same time, Japan expanded its dominance and control over the Marshall and Caroline Islands in the Pacific. While the United States referred to these possessions as Japan's "mandated islands," the Japanese called them "the Imperial Islands of Japan."

Japan proceeded to occupy the aforementioned islands and establish vast agricultural plantations and compounds, most of them associated with the farming of rice, sugar cane, and rubber trees. In addition, they searched for, located, and exploited oil reserves. What concerned the United States and the rest of the world, however, was the suspected Japanese armed forces buildup accompanied by construction of airfields, shipping docks, and more. The islands were being fortified militarily, and leaders of nations around the globe were wondering to what end. The United States was desperately in need of learning what was going on in the mandated islands but had no way of finding out.

With Earhart's announcement of her plan to fly around the world, advisers in the upper echelons of the federal government saw an opportunity to learn more about what was taking place in the Japanese possessions in the Pacific.

During November 1936, the U.S. government agreed to assist Earhart with her around-the-world flight. President Franklin D. Roosevelt directed the chief of naval operations to provide support. A plan was formulated where Earhart, flying east out of Oakland, would land at Honolulu, refuel, and then travel to Howland Island, southwest of Hawaii, where she would again stop for refueling and maintenance. Howland Island was located in the same general area as the Marshall Islands, an area of particular concern for the U.S. government. In departing the island, Earhart could then fly over the Marshalls and other mandated islands and take photographs of any suspected military ports, airfields, compounds, and other installations. To this end, the U.S. Navy immediately undertook the construction of an airfield on Howland Island, a designated refueling station.

· 9 ·

Enter Robert Myers

$\mathcal{D}$uring the Oakland Airport–based preparations for the flight around the world, Earhart met a fifteen-year-old boy named Robert Myers. The Myers family had moved to Oakland the previous year and purchased a house four miles from the airport. When not in school, Myers would walk or hitchhike to the airport and spend the day watching planes take off and land. So common a sight was he that the mechanics, baggage handlers, and other workers called him by his first name and, since he was well behaved and respectful, allowed him to roam freely about the environs.

As Earhart and her crew were involved in plans for the flight, a large section of the airport was closed down to accommodate them. Events such as races and parachute jumps were postponed for the time being, and much of the space was posted off-limits. In spite of that, Myers was still allowed to visit the area and observe the goings-on. In fact, the airport manager, Guy Turner, had grown fond of the boy and enjoyed seeing him around.

Myers met Earhart, along with a number of other well-known pilots, one year earlier at a powder-puff derby held at the airport. When Earhart would take a break in the tiny Oakland Airport coffee shop and Myers happened to wander by, she would buy him an ice cream cone or some other treat. In time, Earhart began treating Myers like a little brother.

Myers also encountered "a man who called himself Fred Noonan." One day Myers stood nearby and watched while Noonan was washing an airplane. Myers noted that the mechanics and others assisting with Earhart's flight preparations called him "Noonan" or "Fred," but Paul Manning told the youth that his name was not Fred at all, but Bill. A mystery involving the two names would surface years later.

Myers noted that Earhart, Noonan, and Mantz spent extended periods of time in the coffee shop in quiet conversation. On occasion, Myers was invited to sit with them, and he would listen to their discussion regarding aerial communications, engines, logistics, and more. Myers's relationship with Earhart was to involve some curious twists years later.

· 10 ·

Oakland to Honolulu

$\mathcal{O}$n March 17, 1937, hundreds of spectators, including Robert Myers, arrived to watch Earhart take off for the Oakland-Honolulu leg of her much-publicized around-the-world attempt. The Electra lifted off at 4:37 p.m. Pacific Standard Time.

The flight was smooth and uneventful until around 2:00 a.m. the next day. Following a remixing of the fuel combinations, it was noticed that the sound of the propellers was out of synch; one was running faster than the other. Earhart worked with the controls for a few seconds in an attempt to correct the problem, but it soon became clear that the right propeller was stuck at 1,600 rpm. The situation was manageable but would need to be corrected on arriving at Honolulu. They would not be able to continue the flight with this problem. Earhart set the Electra down at Wheeler Field at 5:55 a.m.

On landing, Earhart and the Electra's crew were greeted by the press, hundreds of spectators, and a number of military officials. When the photograph sessions and press conferences were finally over, attention turned to the maintenance of the Electra and the correction of the out-of-synch propeller. Mantz reviewed with the maintenance crew all of the plane's problems. These included the issue with the propeller, a generator that was showing a negative charge, spark plugs that needed to be changed for new ones, and an instrument light on the panel that was too bright. It was intended that they take off for Howland Island that evening.

Earhart managed a call to Putnam in Oakland to update him on the status of the flight. She caught him up on the specifics of the difficulties and related that she was impressed by Noonan's navigational skills.

At 2:00 p.m., Mantz went to the hangar where the Electra was being serviced and learned that the right propeller hub was almost completely dry and required a considerable amount of lubrication. To his surprise, the technician pointed out that it had apparently never been oiled prior to takeoff in Oakland. After filling the hub with lubricant, Mantz and the technician checked for leaks and found none.

The generator problem was the result of a blown current limiter fuse and was repaired. The spark plugs had been cleaned, regapped, and reinstalled. The bright instrument light on the panel was painted white to reduce the glare.

Mantz started up the engines and discovered that the right propeller would not move. Concerned, he had both propellers removed and sent to the Hawaiian Air Depot at Luke Field for complete overhauls. He called Earhart and explained what was going on and informed her he could not provide any information on when the overhauls would be completed but hoped they would be ready for a test flight by 7:00 a.m. the next morning.

While in Honolulu, Noonan fell in the bathroom of his hotel room and, according to his dentist, Dr. F. Clifford Phillips, "broke off his upper front teeth." Most who were close to the navigator were convinced that Noonan, who had a history of drinking problems, was inebriated at the time of the accident. The event was a harbinger of things to come.

On Friday, March 19, Earhart and Mantz arrived at Wheeler Field just before 6:00 a.m. and walked into the hangar where the Electra was being worked on. A Lieutenant Arnold greeted them and reviewed the work that had been done on the propellers. Following this, Earhart and Mantz inspected the runway and expressed dissatisfaction with the conditions. As a result of recent construction projects, shallow trenches had been excavated across the takeoff and landing strip and not refilled. Earhart decided to move the plane to nearby Luke Field on Ford Island in Pearl Harbor for the lift-off.

The Electra was fueled and given a preflight inspection. The engines were started. Mantz listened to them for ten minutes before determining they were fit for the flight. Mantz exited the cockpit and walked around the plane examining the engine nacelles and landing gear for leaks. He found none but did notice that the oil- and air-filled shock absorbers, called oleo struts, were out of line. The right one was extended four inches and the left one was extended just over two inches. Mantz summoned the mechanic. He let the air out of the right one, bringing it into line with the left. Mantz finally declared the plane in good condition and informed the officers in charge of the depot that the mechanics had done a stellar job. The Electra was given a test flight from Wheeler Field to Luke Field.

On reexamining the Electra after landing at Luke Field, Mantz noticed that the right oleo strut was extended two and one-eighth inches, the left was extended two and five-eighths inches, and the right strut valve was leaking.

Assisted by a mechanic, Mantz replaced the valve core on the right strut and pumped air into it until it was equal to the left. After more conferences between Mantz, Earhart, and the mechanics, it was decided to take off from Luke Field either at 11:00 p.m. that evening or at dawn of the following day, depending on the weather. Earhart asked Noonan to accompany the flight all the way to Australia, and he agreed to do so.

· 11 ·

The Crash

As a result of a minor problem with a fuel filter and a more serious one with the weather, it was decided to delay the takeoff until the following morning. At 5:30 a.m., Earhart entered the cockpit among cheers from spectators and the popping of flashbulbs. At around 5:40, Earhart taxied to the end of the runway. She advanced the throttles until the engines were running at half power. She released the brakes and advanced the engines up to full power. As the plane moved down the runway, the left engine was running noticeably faster than the right one, and the Electra drifted slightly to the right.

Though accelerating smoothly, the plane continued to drift. In an attempt to steer the plane back to center, Earhart pushed the left rudder pedal hard, but it appeared to have no effect. She then eased the left throttle back to remove some of the power from the left engine. At that moment, the right wing dipped. With the left engine power reduced, the plane began a long left turn while seeming to accelerate—the beginnings of what is termed a ground loop. A ground loop is defined as a "loss of directional control while the aircraft is on the ground." It is similar to a vehicle spinning out. The plane tilted, and the right wing tip scraped the ground. Suddenly, the right landing gear collapsed, to be followed a second later by the left. The Electra went into a left-oriented skid on its belly. To the relief of everyone on board as well as those watching, there was no explosion or fire. Some said it was a miracle.

Numerous explanations were offered for the cause of the ground loop, some of them in relative agreement and others conflicting. Harry Manning was quoted as stating that Earhart was responsible for the crash and that it resulted when she began "jockeying the throttles on takeoff . . . she simply lost it." At this point, Manning claimed he began to have second thoughts about accompanying Earhart on her around-the-world flight. A short time later,

Manning made it clear to everyone that he would not accompany Earhart on her trip when it was tried again.

In support of Manning's contention, Paul Mantz said Earhart "had a tendency to hold runway alignment by jockeying the throttles rather than using the rudder." Mantz implied that the accident was completely Earhart's fault. Putnam bridled at this criticism and began making plans to eliminate Mantz from the flight team.

There were some who held a different perspective relative to the ground loop, suggesting that it was done deliberately. There exists some controversy as to how much gas was pumped into the tanks prior to the takeoff attempt. It has been contended that the tanks held very little fuel. If the aborted attempt had been planned, explosion and fire potential would be minimized with nearly empty fuel tanks. The possibility has also been advanced that it was not Earhart at the controls of the Electra when the ground loop occurred, but Fred Noonan. This, however, has never been verified. Noonan, in truth, was visibly affected by the setback. It was reported that he grew depressed and locked himself in his hotel room.

During the nearly eight decades that have passed since the accident, the notion that the ground loop was deliberate has been proposed by others. Robert Myers stated he was informed by one of his neighbors in Oakland who had been stationed in Honolulu at the time of the accident that when Earhart began her takeoff process, "it looked very odd and the consensus among those who were involved and present at the time was that the takeoff was deliberately aborted."

Aircraft mechanic Arthur Kennedy stated that Earhart was a fine pilot and expressed disbelief regarding the ground loop. He said there was "something fishy" about the event. Kennedy was regarded as one of the top airplane mechanics of the 1930s.

Kennedy also stated that the initial report of the crash was incorrect and misleading. He approached Earhart and told her that her ground loop was not a normal one, that it had clearly been forced. Earhart responded that it was none of Kennedy's business and insisted that he not repeat his observations to anyone. Kennedy reminded Earhart that an inspector was due to arrive the next day and something would have to be done to the airplane.

Visibly irritated, Earhart admonished Kennedy, "You didn't see a thing. We'll just force the gear back over to make it look natural." She then exacted a promise from Kennedy not to say anything about the crash. Kennedy agreed, and he kept his secret until 1992, when he related the experience in his book, *High Times: Keeping 'Em Flying*.

Later, when the airline mechanics quit for the day and left for home, Kennedy and Earhart "jacked up the wing off the floor and reset the right landing gear using an eight-foot pry bar. While they were working, Earhart explained to Kennedy that while she was in the Electra making preparations to take off, she received instructions that she must abort the flight. She refused to tell Kennedy who issued the order.

In his book, Kennedy also related an incident wherein Earhart and Mantz were involved in a heated discussion, with a furious Mantz telling Earhart that the Electra could not possibly ground loop at takeoff speed.

Later, Earhart invited Kennedy and his wife out to dinner. During the meal, Earhart appeared very nervous and upset and explained to Kennedy that a lot depended on him keeping his silence regarding his interpretation of the ground loop. Earhart told him that "she was on a secret mission that had to look like a normal civilian flight."

The obvious question is: Why would Earhart deliberately cause the Electra to crash? A number of answers have been offered over the years, but the one advanced that carries with it some logic and fits all aspects of the circumstances is: with the damage done to the plane—and it was somewhat minimal—it provided a reason for the craft to be shipped back to Oakland and to the Lockheed factory at Burbank, where it could be repaired but also refitted specifically for the secretive purposes attached to Earhart's around-the-world flight.

Author Randall Brink wrote that after Earhart ground-looped the Electra, "the Navy and Coast Guard completely took over the flight. Amelia . . . made no decisions anymore, and we had no contact with her." During his research, Brink located a memo from President Franklin D. Roosevelt "in which he tacitly ordered the U. S. Navy to assist on Earhart's flight." In truth, it went beyond that; the government offered to subsidize Earhart's flight around the world in return for full control of the project. Earhart agreed.

· 12 ·

A Visit from Washington

$\mathscr{B}$ased on some compelling evidence, a number of researchers are convinced that, during the spring of 1937, President Roosevelt summoned one of his special advisers, Bernard Baruch, to enlist the assistance of U.S. Army Air Corps Major General Oscar Westover and travel to California, meet with Amelia Earhart, and convince her of the need for her participation in the plans to gather intelligence via her planned flight.

A short time after meeting with the president, Baruch and Westover traveled by train to the home of Earhart and Putnam in Toluca Lake, California, to conduct a series of three meetings. According to Earhart's personal secretary, Margot DeCarie, Baruch and Westover arrived during the middle of April 1937. DeCarie states that it was between Earhart's Honolulu ground loop and the undertaking of her second attempt of the around-the-world flight. Each meeting, she says, lasted three to four hours in length and was held under secrecy at March Army Air Corps Field in Riverdale, California, ninety miles from the home of Earhart and Putnam. So secret were these meetings that Baruch and Westover insisted Putnam be kept away, which infuriated him. Although she was never informed of any details, DeCarie learned that one of the outcomes of the meetings led to a significant change of plans relative to Earhart's around-the-world flight.

The United States was in need of information relative to Japanese military buildup in the mandated islands of the Pacific, particularly the Marshall Islands. The islands were named after the British navigator John Marshall, who visited them in 1798. Spain claimed ownership, but Germany took possession of them in 1886. During World War I, the Japanese occupied the islands and thereafter claimed ownership. Earhart's around-the-world flight would provide the perfect cover for a reconnaissance of them.

Earhart researcher Rollin C. Reineck advances the notion that plans were made for Earhart to take off from Howland Island and then feign an emergency. She was to report engine trouble and would send distress signals stating that she was in the area of the Marshall Islands. Following this, Earhart would cease radio transmissions and proceed toward the island of Nilhau, the northernmost island of the Hawaiian group, where a landing field had recently been constructed. There, she and Noonan would remain in hiding until the U.S. Navy completed its search for them. In response to her distress signals, the U.S. Navy would dispatch ships and aircraft to the area around the Marshall Islands under the guise of looking for Noonan and her.

The government assumed that the Japanese would not object to a search-and-rescue effort in the area of the Marshall Islands. Should the imperial leaders refuse, U.S. thinking was that they would soon succumb to world pressure. Following a sweep of the Marshalls, the United States would then announce the rescue of Earhart and Noonan and surreptitiously deliver them to Honolulu.

During an interview conducted in November 1966 and published in the *San Fernando Valley Times*, DeCarie stated that she knew Earhart "was working for the government." In addition to the meetings with Baruch and Westover, Earhart also met with other government agents at the Toluca Lake home. DeCarie and Putnam were never permitted to be part of these meetings. During the interviews, DeCarie stated: "To me it looked like she was supposed to get lost on the theory that the Japanese would allow a peace mission to search for her. Then the United States could see if the Japanese were fortifying the . . . islands in violation of mutual agreements." Author David K. Bowman writes that Earhart, "due to her great celebrity and the high esteem in which she was held everywhere, could be expected to go from coast to coast without difficulty or arousing suspicion." Earhart's flight, claims Bowman, "provided the perfect pretext for a covert pre-war global mapping and reconnaissance effort."

The plan seemed sound. Fate, however, was to intrude and throw the entire Earhart around-the-world attempt into a deeper series of mysteries.

· 13 ·

Repairs

$\mathscr{T}$he damage to the Electra rendered it unsuitable for flying: The right wing would need to be replaced; the right engine and nacelle were nearly torn away; the oleo struts were useless; at least one tire had blown; the right oil tank had burst; the fuel filter neck had been torn open. The fuel was drained from the tanks, and the plane was towed back to the hangar. Plans were already being made to have the plane transported back to the Lockheed factory at Burbank for repairs. When Earhart finally was able to contact Putnam about the incident, he told her to write a first-hand account of the crash and he would get it in all of the newspapers. Most of what the American public learned about Earhart's crash was the structured press release designed by Putnam and written by Earhart.

With Mantz handling the arrangements, the Army Air Corps prepared the Electra for shipment. It was to be moved from Luke Field and transported across the ocean to a port at San Pedro, California.

The repairs necessitated by the crash of the Electra represented a financial setback for Earhart and Putnam. The cost of the repairs was beyond their current means, so Putnam busied himself with lining up sponsors again. One of his first pleas was to the Purdue University benefactors, several of whom came through with assistance.

While plans were being made for the repairs to the Electra, Earhart met with Manning and informed him that he was to be replaced by Fred Noonan as navigator. Later, Manning stated that he quit the around-the-world enterprise because he had "lost faith in Earhart's skill as a pilot and was fed up with her bullheadedness." Author Elgen Long reports that Manning was "gentlemanly" about the dismissal and would return to his responsibilities as a ship captain at the first opportunity.

The Electra was loaded as deck cargo onto the SS *Lurline*. The total cost to Earhart and Putnam for crating the aircraft and preparing it for transport, for storage, and for other expenses totaled $5,200.

According to a newspaper report, the Electra arrived at San Pedro Harbor on April 2, was off-loaded, and was collected by the Smith Brothers Trucking Company. The plane arrived at the Lockheed factory in Burbank on Sunday afternoon. Following a thorough inspection, Putnam was informed that the cost of repairs to the aircraft would be approximately $12,000. Putnam instructed them to proceed.

During the repairs, Earhart requested that the trailing wire antenna be removed. Radioman Joe Gurr decided to attach an antenna mast on the top of the fuselage as a replacement for the trailing wire setup.

The only exit on the right side of the Electra was an escape hatch over the wing. Because of the fuselage fuel tanks that had been installed, this hatch was rendered useless. A new exit was fashioned by replacing the lavatory window with a hatch.

The two engines had been removed, disassembled, and completely inspected. Each of the propellers had to be replaced, but the propeller hubs were deemed to be in good condition. It was estimated that the Electra would be ready to fly in a month.

As the repairs to the Electra continued, the money to finance them was slow in arriving. Putnam, ever the entrepreneur who was experienced in getting people to respond, drafted a letter to one of the principal sponsors and a Purdue benefactor whose contribution was late. Putnam informed the sponsor, as well as the president of Purdue, that Earhart's story of the flight would be carried in thirty-eight major newspapers around the world and that sponsors would be prominently mentioned.

By the middle of May, the Electra was ready for testing. As Gurr briefed Earhart on the operation of the radio equipment he had installed, it became clear to him that she was hesitant about using it. Further, she had not taken the time to familiarize herself with the new Bendix receiver.

As ground and flight testing of the Electra proceeded, Earhart, after studying weather charts and determining that she did not want to fly into the patterns that existed this time of the year, considered that it might be best to orient her flight from west to east instead of the original east-to-west plan. The Pacific portion of the flight would thus become the last leg of the trip rather than the first.

By the time the Electra had undergone complete repairs and modifications, the total cost was estimated to be around $25,000. A $20,000 contribution from Vincent Bendix of Bendix Radio arrived, as did a check for $10,000 from Floyd Odlum, Jackie Cochran's husband. Curiously, a donation arrived from Bernard Baruch, an adviser to President Franklin D. Roosevelt.

On May 20, 1937, Earhart flew the Electra from Burbank to Oakland. From Oakland, she decided, she would soon begin her second attempt at the around-the-world flight, but she withheld a public announcement of her plans.

The Coast Guard cutter *Shoshone* left Honolulu in May bound for Howland Island, where it would deposit thirty-one drums of flight fuel and two barrels of lubrication oil ostensibly for the Electra. The U.S. Navy tug *Ontario* was scheduled to leave American Samoa as soon as it took on fuel and supplies. The tug would monitor Earhart's flight and assist when necessary.

A bit of a mystery surrounds the repair of the Electra. When the craft was returned to Oakland, it was placed in a remote section of the airfield far from the runways. Robert Myers claimed that while newspapers were reporting that the plane had been shipped to Burbank, it was, in fact, parked at the airfield in Oakland, covered by a large tarp, and placed some distance away from the runways such that the mechanics and technicians who were working on it had to drive their vehicles from the hangar to the plane. The craft was under around-the-clock security, and no unauthorized personnel were allowed near it. According to Myers, a crew of three mechanics worked on the plane twenty-four hours per day.

All of the factory electronics had been stripped out of it, including the radio. Myers knew the crew members and would listen to their conversations in the coffee shop from time to time. He heard one of them mention that they had removed all of the wiring and radio equipment, all to be replaced with new specifications. All of the work was conducted under tight security, and the tarp was never removed from the aircraft. On one occasion, Myers claimed, he heard Harry Manning state that they were doing things to the Electra that he had never seen done before. Before he departed after being released by Earhart and Putnam, Manning made the comment, "Something is funny about this flight."

At one point, the Electra was towed into the nearest hangar. Days later, as Myers was sitting in the coffee shop, he spotted the Electra's fuselage strapped onto the bed of a large truck. The wings were strapped down alongside the body of the craft, and the wheels had been removed. The truck stopped outside the coffee shop and the driver entered, ordered a cup to go, and was preparing to leave when Myers asked him where he was taking the plane. He said it was to be delivered to Burbank. Myers presumed it was going to the Lockheed factory and said as much. The driver told Myers he couldn't say any more because it was all "top secret."

The entire business of repairs being conducted on the Electra has given rise to another series of mysteries. During a visit to the airport ten days later, Myers noticed that the Electra had been returned and reassembled. It was parked near the hangar and was being washed down. On closer inspection, however, Myers became convinced it was not the same airplane, noting that a number of features were significantly different from the plane that he had seen earlier. Where the Electra had earlier sported a loop-style navigation antenna, it now had a navigational bubble located farther aft on the fuselage. The reconfigured aircraft had different navigational lights. The engine cowlings were either different or had been painted. The door to the navigator's compartment was also different. The plane that had been sent off to Burbank for repairs had a door with a window in it, but the one that was returned had a door with no window. Some have argued that these were simply modifications made to the original aircraft, but Myers was not so certain.

A Lockheed Aircraft Company mechanic named Robert T. Elliot, who was interviewed years later, stated that he did modifications on the aircraft to allow the installation of two Fairchild aerial survey cameras. He was quoted as saying that the business of repairing the Electra "was just a ruse."

Carroll F. Harris, a Navy clerk who had been assigned to transfer secret Earhart files to microfilm, recalled seeing the "complete details, along with photographs, of the installation and operation of the Fairchild aerial survey cameras in the belly of the [Electra]." Harris also stated that the files contained information on modifications of the aircraft's electrical system "so that it could handle the increased load placed in it by the surveillance cameras."

Lloyd Royer, another Lockheed mechanic who worked on the Electra, said that "the plane in which Earhart departed on her second attempt was different from the one used in the original attempt." Royer implied that the Electra had not been repaired but that it had been replaced.

When Earhart arrived at the airport from Los Angeles, she took one look at the Electra and, according to Myers, said, "Why did they have to do this to my plane? I loved my old plane. Who is paying for this?" Later Myers heard Noonan mention that the new aircraft would have a lot more power. Much to his amazement, Myers also learned that every empty space and every compartment in the new plane had been filled with ping-pong balls. This was not a novel procedure. Prior to an earlier long-distance flight over open water by pilot Henry T. "Dick" Merrill, his plane had been filled with ping-pong balls to provide for greater buoyancy should the plane have the misfortune of coming down on the water.

In 1982, Myers interviewed a former Lockheed employee, Rollo Christy, who had been assigned to work on Earhart's plane when it had been returned to the factory. Cristy said he had been given the job of adding the ping-pong balls. Christy also mentioned observing a lot of "sophisticated camera equipment" that had been installed in the Electra. Once while wandering around the hangar, Myers spotted several boxes of camera film that were marked for loading into the Electra. In addition, he saw a large camera that had a U.S. Navy insignia on it.

Years later it was learned that around this time, Army Air Corp Corporal Joseph Pelligrini was assigned to the first photo mapping group at Bolling Field, Washington, D.C. Pelligrini's assignment was to draw up the guidelines for installing cameras in a "civilian aircraft to be flown by a female pilot engaged in an intelligence flight." According to Pelligrini, a female pilot was to take photographs of Japanese mandated islands in the Pacific Ocean.

Days later while seated at a table in the coffee shop with Earhart and Noonan, Myers witnessed the aviatrix yelling at her navigator and asking him what he knew about all of the camera equipment that had been added to the airplane. She asked him, "Why is [Putnam] doing all of this? Why won't he tell me a thing?" Noonan responded that he was in the dark about the entire matter.

Myers noticed Putnam coming and going at the airport more often as the time approached for the around-the-world flight. Myers came to the conclusion that Putnam was in charge of the entire enterprise, that he was making all of the decisions related to the flight. Myers found Putnam to be "a most disagreeable person" and observed him behaving in an abusive manner toward his son.

During another visit to the coffee shop, Myers overheard a conversation between Earhart and Noonan wherein she commented that she knew her husband was up to something and that he wouldn't tell her anything, that he wouldn't even talk to her anymore.

On one occasion, Myers reported that as he was walking home from the coffee shop, he "saw Putnam hitting his son . . . and yelling at him for leaving the parked car." He claimed that on seeing him, Putnam pushed his son aside and approached Myers, angry. Putnam demanded to know what Manning and Earhart had told him in the coffee shop. Before Myers could reply, Putnam yelled, "You've heard and seen a lot of things you were not supposed to, kid, haven't you?" Myers continued walking away but Putnam screamed at him to stay away from the airport. Myers then stated that Putnam said, "You'd better stay away from here. I don't want to see you around here again. If I catch you around here again, you will disappear and no one will know where to find you."

As a young boy, Myers was unaware of the import of what he heard and observed. His recollections of that period, however, would contribute to unraveling one or more of the mysteries that were beginning to surround Amelia Earhart and would continue to do so long after her disappearance.

Over the years, a number of Earhart enthusiasts have been critical of Robert Myers's accounts regarding the aviatrix, in large part because those accounts differed from the critics' own points of view. For a time, Myers became defensive about the criticism and refused to talk about his relationship with Earhart. Then, as an adult, he subjected himself to a series of lie detector tests. The results indicated he was not making up any of his stories.

· 14 ·

Fred Noonan

From all outward appearances, it seemed as though Fred Noonan was the ideal partner to accompany Amelia Earhart on her planned around-the-world flight. For those intimate with Noonan and his history, however, his selection as navigator was a surprise to many and has caused numerous questions to be raised over the years.

Noonan was forty-four years old at the time of the preparations for the flight. Noonan claimed to have been born in Chicago, but no record of such has ever been found. Allegedly, he attended public schools in Chicago as well as a private military academy. The name of the academy is unknown. In addition, he claimed to have studied at the London Nautical College. Documents to support these contentions have never been found.

Noonan joined the navy at seventeen years of age and spent twenty-two years as a merchant sailor and officer. He survived the sinking of three ships struck by German U-boat torpedoes during World War I. Noonan earned a master's license for oceangoing ships of unlimited tonnage. Later, he qualified for a license as a Mississippi River boat pilot.

Noonan eventually quit the sea and moved into aviation. While living in New Orleans in 1929, he took flight training at the Texas Air Transport SAT division in nearby Chalmette. In January 1930, he was issued a pilot's license for transport planes. In 1930, he started working for the New York, Rio, and Buenos Aires Airlines that later merged into Pan American Airways. In 1935, Noonan navigated the first round trip of the four-engine flying boat, the *China Clipper*, between San Francisco and Honolulu. Later, he mapped Pan American clipper routes across the Pacific Ocean. In 1934, he was assigned to the newly established Pan Am Pacific Division, headquartered in San Francisco.

No one doubted Noonan's abilities as a navigator. In truth, he was famous, almost legendary, among navigators for his pioneering Pan American Airways work and was regarded as the most accomplished aerial navigator in the world. He soon earned a reputation as being competent with the complexities of celestial navigation and in a short time was regarded as one of the most experienced navigators in the world—when he was sober. Though never noted in his military and professional records, it was well known that Noonan had a drinking problem.

In spite of his numerous and documented successes at Pan Am, the "official" story was that he resigned from the company after seven years. Another version of his departure from Pan Am, and likely the true one, had to do with Noonan's well-known drinking problem; the company was forced to let him go. According to author Vincent Loomis, "No one in the aviation industry would touch him . . . because of his addiction to alcohol." As it happened, Noonan was living in Oakland as Earhart and her team were preparing for the flight around the world.

At one time or another, Putnam, Mantz, and Earhart all expressed some dissatisfaction with the navigational abilities of Manning. William Miller of the Bureau of Air Commerce asked Putnam how the Oakland-to-Honolulu flight had gone, and Putnam commented on concerns relative to Manning's navigational problems. Miller told Putnam about Noonan, praised him highly, and suggested that he could set up a meeting between the two men. A conference was arranged a few days later, and by the time it was concluded, Noonan had agreed to assist in the navigation as far as Howland Island. Earhart met with Noonan a short time later. With the passage of a few more days, he would be selected to replace Manning as navigator.

As preparations continued for the around-the-world flight, Noonan was filing for a Mexican divorce from his wife. Approximately one week later, he and his fiancée, Mary B. "Bee" Martinelli, eloped to Yuma, Arizona, and were married on March 27. Noonan and Bee were driving the Golden Gate Highway near Fresno on the way back to Oakland, Fred at the wheel, when they experienced a head-on collision. The subsequent investigation showed Noonan was driving in the wrong lane of traffic. Acquaintances suspected Noonan was drunk.

At the time, Noonan held a second-class commercial radio operator's license that he had earned around 1931. This type of license required "transmitting and sound reading at a speed not less than sixteen words per minute in Continental Morse Code and twenty words per minute in plain language." In 1935, Almon Gray, a Pan American Airways flight officer, observed that Noonan could send and receive plain language at speeds of only eight to ten words per minute. Ultimately, it was determined Noonan had limited facility with Morse code.

Some confusion exists today over whether or not Noonan held military rank during the around-the-world attempt. A letter from the Office of the Chief of Naval Operations dated December 29, 1960, dealing with the Earhart disappearance referred to "Commander Noonan, her navigator." Other references to Noonan in the Earhart literature refer to him as Captain Noonan, and some insist he was a reserve officer in the U.S. Navy. Still others suggest Noonan may have been assigned to active duty prior to the flight with Earhart and was, in fact, under orders from the U.S. military. While a provocative suggestion, it has never been proved.

· 15 ·

Reenter Putnam

$\mathcal{G}$eorge Palmer Putnam was ubiquitous at the Oakland airport. From time to time he received visitors who appeared to be officials or dignitaries of some kind whom he would escort to the hangar where the Electra was being worked on. On those occasions, Putnam would order all of the mechanics and technicians out of the building and tell them not to return until he informed them it was all right to do so. Even Earhart was instructed to leave on occasion. During these mysterious visits, the aviatrix would generally retreat to the coffee shop and visit with Noonan and Mantz.

Once as he was passing by the table where the three sat in conversation, young Robert Myers overheard Earhart ask of Noonan and Mantz whether they knew who the visitors were and what they thought Putnam was up to. Neither of the two men had any idea.

During one visit to the airport, Myers walked up on Earhart, Noonan, and Mantz as the latter was showing the aviatrix some camera gear and providing basic instructions on aerial photography.

On another visit to the airport, Myers observed Putnam grow exceedingly angry with his young son because he "had not washed up well enough." Putnam yelled at the boy and then hit him. On one other occasion when Myers was seated in the coffee shop near Earhart and Noonan, he heard the aviatrix state, "I don't care what they tell you, Fred. There is something going on and they are not telling you and they are not telling me. [Putnam] won't tell me a thing and I know he is up to something. He won't even talk to me anymore."

Referring to a number of government officials who had been coming and going at the airport, Earhart asked Noonan whether he knew who they were. He didn't. Given the growing and suspicious nature of such activities, Earhart offered Noonan an opportunity to back out of the flight. He declined.

At one point when Robert Myers was in the coffee shop, Earhart told him she needed to tell him something. According to Myers, Earhart said, "I am on a very secret and dangerous mission and I want you to tell someone if you hear that anything happens to Fred or me, tell your mother or someone else." Earhart made Myers promise he would.

Later, as Myers was leaving the coffee shop, he spotted Putnam screaming at his son and hitting him again. The offense committed by the boy that angered Putnam this time had to do with leaving the parked car, where he had been instructed to remain. Putnam saw Myers watching him. He pushed his son aside and advanced toward Myers, an angry snarl on his face. On reaching Myers, Putnam asked him what they had told him in the coffee shop. Myers walked away, with Putnam screaming at him to stay away from the airport.

In what seems like a far-fetched account, Myers reported that as he was walking home along the road, hoping to hitch a ride, a car approached and he stuck out his thumb. As the vehicle neared, it picked up speed. A moment later, Myers recognized the car as the black Hudson owned by Putnam. Putnam was behind the wheel and was aiming at the youth standing on the side of the road. Myers jumped into an adjacent ditch just in time as the car sped by. When he crawled out of the ditch, he watched as Putnam turned the Hudson around for a second attempt at running him down. At this time, however, another car approached, and Myers waved his arms for it to stop. When it did, he climbed in and left the scene.

The incidents between Robert Myers and Putnam represent an odd layer of intrigue associated with Earhart's around-the-world flight, one of many more to come.

· 16 ·

Flight around the World: Second Attempt

$\mathcal{A}$s preparations were being made for the second attempt at a flight around the world, Earhart formally announced she had replaced Manning with Fred Noonan as navigator. By this time she had made a final determination on a different route from the one originally planned. Because of the changing seasons she was now forced to accommodate variations in climatic conditions.

Prior to taking off, Earhart handed her secretary, Margot DeCarie, a large manila envelope and told her, "If I don't come back, destroy it without opening it." To this day, no one has any inkling as to what the envelope contained.

Earhart, accompanied by Noonan, took off from Oakland at 3:50 p.m. on May 20, 1937, in her second bid to become the first woman to fly around the world. Curiously, and in a major departure from previous flights, no announcements were made and thus no throngs of press and onlookers were at the airport to observe the liftoff. Two hours and ten minutes later the Electra landed in Burbank, where Bo McNeely was waiting to service the plane. McNeely, along with Putnam, were to accompany Earhart and Noonan to Miami. From there, Putnam would proceed on to New York, where he would stay until Earhart reached and then departed Australia. At that time he would fly to Oakland to make preparations for her return. Putnam was still busy trying to raise additional sponsors but was having limited success. He was forced to mortgage his house in order to raise enough money to finance expenses for the flight.

Earhart, Noonan, Putnam, and McNeely left Union Air Terminal at Burbank at 2:25 p.m. and landed at Tucson three hours and twenty minutes later. The left engine had experienced backfires during the flight, was serviced, and was determined to be in fine working order. The four spent the

49

night at the Pioneer Hotel and departed the next morning, May 22, at 7:30 a.m. and arrived in New Orleans eight hours and forty minutes later. After spending the night, they left for Miami, Florida, at 9:10 a.m. CST. Most of this portion of the flight was across the open water of the Gulf of Mexico, and Noonan's navigation proved effective. They landed in Miami at 3:04 p.m. EST.

Earhart reported that the autopilot's rudder control was not working and that the radio transmitter was not functioning. Pan American Airways sent a crew of mechanics and technicians to the Miami airport to work on the plane. Earhart was asked how the 500-kilocycle communications had worked, and she replied that she had not used that frequency. She also volunteered that neither she nor Noonan understood Morse code well enough to send or receive on the instrument. The autopilot was declared fixed and the radios examined, tested, and deemed in good working order.

Some Earhart researchers have claimed that it was during the stop in Miami that Earhart had the trailing wire antenna removed from the Electra. Evidence exists, however, that she more likely had it removed while the craft was at the Lockheed factory in Burbank for repairs.

It was in Miami that Earhart officially announced she had begun her around-the-world flight and that she would be flying from west to east as a result of weather considerations. She commented that she would not use the Morse code wireless set that had been installed in the plane and that she would rely entirely on voice transmissions and receptions on 3,105 and 6,210 kilocycles. A subsequent examination revealed that the once-repaired autopilot was still not functioning properly.

When Paul Mantz learned of Earhart's departure, he was attending an aerobatic competition in St. Louis. He was described as being furious and quoted as stating that Earhart "was not ready" and that he "smelled disaster." Mantz explained that Earhart had been "pushed too hard, trying to meet the tight schedules set up by her promoter husband." Mantz claimed too much attention had been given to the moneymaking schemes, advertising gimmicks, books, screenplays, public appearances, and endorsements.

Earhart and Noonan remained in Miami for more than a week while Bo McNeely and Pan American mechanics worked on the aircraft to make certain it was in condition for the long flight. One of the mechanics recalled closing the cowling on one of the engines and not yet having wiped away his greasy handprints. When Earhart walked out to the flight line to inspect the work, she spotted the mess and cursed the worker with words the mechanic said he "didn't believe any woman even knew!"

Mantz, who remained in contact with several of the Pan American mechanics, was stunned when he learned that Earhart had decided to leave the telegraph key and the trailing wire antenna behind. Mantz believed Earhart was taking a risky chance without the equipment.

Author, explorer, and pilot Bradford Washburn also expressed amazement at Earhart's refusal to use the communication devices Mantz had installed in the Electra. He explained how this greatly reduced the range of her reception and that "by having that terribly short antenna system, she vastly reduced the number of people who might conceivably pick her up." This limited ability to communicate was to generate problems in a short time.

Finally, the Electra departed Miami on June 1 at 5:56 a.m. EST for San Juan, Puerto Rico, where it arrived seven hours and thirty-four minutes later. Once again, a great part of the flight was over open water, and Noonan's navigational skills proved adept. The following morning they lifted off before dawn, their destination being Caripito in Venezuela, on the northern coast of South America. It took them four hours and thirty-two minutes from Puerto Rico. Strong headwinds and heavy rains forced a delay, and Earhart and Noonan stayed overnight at the residence of Standard Oil Company's general manager.

The manager of the Pan American station at Caripito was Harry Drake, an old friend of Fred Noonan. Drake told Earhart and Noonan that he would meet with them in the morning just before takeoff with the latest weather and airport information. According to author Vincent Loomis, Earhart brushed off Drake with a curt, "I don't need any of that stuff. I got it back in California before I left." Drake was stunned at the response and explained that her information was already out of date. As he watched the Electra lift off, he wondered whether he would ever see Earhart and Noonan alive again.

That morning, they took off at 8:48 a.m. Venezuelan time, bound for Paramaribo, Dutch Guiana (today called Suriname). This leg of the flight took four hours and fifty minutes.

The next stop was Fortaleza, Brazil, 1,300 miles away. They departed at 7:10 a.m. and flew for nine hours and twenty minutes, landing at 5:00 p.m., Brazilian Eastern Time. At Fortaleza, Earhart reported that the overhead hatch was leaking water when they flew through rain, and the Pan American maintenance crew went straight to work to fix the problem as well as provide the necessary routine maintenance and service.

Earhart and Noonan spent the night at the Excelsior Hotel. They departed the Fortaleza airport at 6:50 a.m. for Natal, Brazil. Earhart paid special attention to the airplane's functions, since on leaving Natal the following day they would be flying nonstop across the Atlantic Ocean. The flight took two hours and five minutes. On arriving in Natal, Earhart inquired about the weather and was told that the next reliable reports would arrive around midnight. She decided to wait but expressed her impatience with the delay.

While the Electra was being serviced, Noonan conveyed a need for some drinks to relieve what author Loomis reported as "unjustifiable pushing" from Earhart. To those who observed the pilot and navigator, there appeared to be a growing tension between them.

At 3:13 a.m. the next morning, June 7, they departed the Natal airport, bound for Dakar in the country of Senegal on the western coast of Africa. It would be the first time a female pilot had ever made this transatlantic crossing.

During the flight, Earhart tried listening in on the Bendix receiver but determined it was not working and therefore useless for navigation. In addition, one of the fuel flow meters ceased operating. Noonan's navigation had placed them a few miles north of their destination when they reached the west coast of Africa. With a directional adjustment, they located and landed at the Saint-Louis airfield. Saint-Louis was an island just off the coast of and belonging to the confederation of French West Africa, which included Senegal. Touchdown was at 7:35 p.m. local time. It had taken thirteen hours and twenty-two minutes to make the Atlantic crossing.

The next morning they flew on to Dakar's Ouakam Airport, 120 miles away. There, the engines were given a standard forty-hour servicing. The fuel flow meter was repaired and reinstalled. A field test showed everything was working properly.

On Thursday, June 10, at 6:51 a.m. Dakar time, Earhart and Noonan took off headed for Gao, the first of four stops across the interior of Africa. They landed at Gao at 2:46 p.m. Greenwich Mean Time. Gao is located precisely on the Greenwich prime meridian. The plane was fueled and oiled. The next morning, they departed eastward toward Fort Lamy at 6:10 a.m. GMT. They landed at Fort Lamy after six hours and thirty-eight minutes of flight.

A few hours prior to Earhart lifting off, the U.S. Coast Guard cutter *Itasca* was ordered to begin preparations to proceed to Howland Island by way of Honolulu.

During a preflight inspection on Saturday morning, June 12, Earhart discovered that one of the oleo shock absorber struts was leaking air. A necessary valve was replaced. Around 10:00 a.m., Earhart decided it was too late to try to make their next stop, Khartoum, before sundown. She decided instead to fly to El Fasher, which was located five hundred miles west of Khartoum. El Fasher was only 695 miles away. Khartoum was more than 1,100 miles away. She and Noonan took off at 12:24 p.m. As usual, using celestial navigation and dead reckoning, Noonan navigated competently across the sandy wastes of the Sahara Desert, and four hours and six minutes later they landed at El Fasher, Darfur Province.

The next morning, June 13, they took off at 6:10 a.m. Without incident or navigational problems, they landed at the Khartoum Aerodrome after three hours and fifteen minutes. The following morning at 10:50 a.m. they departed for Massawa. During the flight, they passed a short distance north of Asmara, the capital of Eritrea, in the horn of Africa. Asmara was regarded as a strategic location by the British, who needed intelligence on this facility.

According to author James Donahue, a former engineer and consultant with the Lockheed and Northrop aviation companies, Earhart had instructions to take clandestine photographs of the airport at Asmara. Donahue claimed evidence exists to suggest that when she landed at the Royal Air Force base at Khartoum, a camera and film were installed in her plane in a compartment under the flight deck. After landing in Karachi, claims Donahue, the film and camera were removed by Royal Air Force personnel. Earhart and Noonan landed at the Otumlo Airdrome in Massawa following a flight of two hours and fifty minutes.

At Massawa the oil was changed and the plane thoroughly inspected and serviced. At this point, Earhart made a decision to fly to Assab, Eritrea, about three hundred miles to the southeast on the coast of the Red Sea. In addition, it would be three hundred miles closer to their next stop—Karachi, India (now Pakistan). At 7:30 a.m. Eritrean time on the morning of June 14, Earhart lifted off the Electra and followed the coast of the Red Sea to Assab. She landed at an Italian military airfield at 9:56 a.m.

While at Assab, Noonan wrote a letter to his wife. Among other things, he informed her that the maps and charts they had been supplied with were misleading and incomplete. The next morning, June 15, the Electra lifted off at 3:15 a.m. During the flight, Earhart was having trouble with the fuel flow meter again. In addition, she had problems with the exhaust analyzer, which assisted with fuel mixture and economy. After thirteen hours and twenty-two minutes, the Electra touched down at the Drigh Road Civil Aerodrome in Karachi. While Earhart and Noonan were spending the night in Karachi, the *Itasca* had reached Honolulu and was setting out for Howland Island.

In the airport hangar, the plane was serviced, the oil changed, and new spark plugs installed. There were technicians available to examine and test the communications systems on board the Electra, but they got no instructions from Earhart. The Cambridge exhaust analyzer was not functioning, and there were no spare parts available for repair. Earhart sent a telegram to Putnam explaining the problem and requested he have a replacement shipped to their next destination. She did not want to attempt crossing the Pacific Ocean without being able to accurately predict how much fuel they were burning. The next morning, June 17, at 7:25 a.m., they departed for Calcutta, India. Following another uneventful flight, they landed in Calcutta at 4:45 p.m.

Shortly after landing, Earhart learned that the KLM Dutch affiliate would be able to repair the Cambridge fuel analyzer, which would be waiting for her at Bandoeng, Java (now Bandung, Indonesia).

The next morning, following a night of heavy rain, Earhart rose early to examine the airfield. She found it saturated with moisture and too soft for an efficient takeoff. She also considered that it was the beginning of the monsoon season, and the field would likely not get any better for a long time. She lifted off without incident at 7:05 a.m., June 18, barely clearing the edge of the forest at the end of the runway. She landed at the Akyab, Burma, airport at 10:00 a.m. After refueling, she took off just after noon. Immediately, Earhart and Noonan encountered heavy rains and were forced to return. They would be forced to wait to see what the next day's conditions were like before attempting another takeoff. The battling with the bad weather was taking a toll on both Earhart and Noonan.

The following morning, June 19, they managed to depart at 6:30 a.m. Once in the air, however, they realized the rain had not diminished from the day before. They were forced to return once again, landing at 7:37 a.m. After examining the charts, Earhart and Noonan decided they could climb to an altitude higher than the coastal mountains and fly over them to Rangoon, their next stop. They took off again at 8:42 a.m. They managed to climb through the heavy rain and turbulence to 8,000 feet, turned to cross the mountains, and made their way to Rangoon, landing during a storm.

After spending the night, Earhart and Noonan returned to the airfield and lifted off at 6:30 a.m., June 20, and landed at Bangkok two hours and forty minutes later. After refueling and subjecting to a quick customs check, they were back in the air by 10:27 a.m. bound for Singapore, nine hundred miles away. During this part of the journey, the fuel flow meters failed again.

Six and one-half hours after leaving Bangkok, the Electra touched down at the Kallang Airport in Singapore. Following a stay with the U.S. consul general in Singapore, Monnet B. Davis, Earhart and Noonan got an early start for Bandoeng on the island of Java. They landed four hours and twenty minutes later. Mechanics went straight to work on the faulty fuel flow instrument and servicing the plane. Earhart explained that she wanted all of the work completed so that she could take off early the next day for Port Darwin, Australia. Later, the mechanics informed Earhart that the work would not be completed in time for her to take off in the morning.

As the mechanics were working on the Electra, the U.S. Navy seaplane tender *Swan* departed Honolulu to establish a position between there and Howland Island to serve as a guard station for Earhart.

Tuesday morning, June 22, Earhart and Noonan arrived at the hangar to check on the progress with the Electra. The mechanics told her that they were certain the plane would be ready for flight on Wednesday morning. However, the next day when Earhart and Noonan arrived early, the mechanics were still working on the engine exhaust stack where the exhaust analyzer had broken. Work was going slowly, so Earhart decided to plan on taking off on Thursday morning.

Noonan was having difficulty bearing up under Earhart's aggressive schedule and sought more relief in alcohol. Earhart placed a call to Putnam. Putnam had no sooner answered his telephone than Earhart blurted out, "He's hitting the bottle again and I don't even know where he's getting it!" She said her patience with her navigator was "wearing thin."

As the plane was being worked on, the *Itasca* arrived at a point just off the eastern side of Howland Island.

At 3:45 a.m. on Thursday morning, Earhart and Noonan climbed into the airplane and started the engines. She tested the exhaust analyzer and the fuel flow meters and discovered that one of the meters was still not working. She summoned the mechanics, and they went back to work on it. By the time they got finished with the repairs, it was too late to undertake the flight to their next scheduled destination, Koepang (Kupang) on the island of Timor, so she decided instead to fly to Surabaya, a Javanese city 360 miles to the west.

Earhart and Noonan arrived at Surabaya at 4:35 p.m. Java time. The next morning as Earhart was preparing for a predawn takeoff, she discovered the oft-repaired fuel flow meter was still not working properly. Earhart placed a call to F. O. Furman, the field engineer at Bandoeng, asking him for advice. Furman recommended she return to Bandoeng, as it was the only place within thousands of miles that was capable of making the necessary repairs. She flew back to Bandoeng, where, some believe, the mechanics found the wiring in the fuel flow meter system had broken. Furman assured Earhart that the instrument could be repaired but that the job could not be completed in time for her to take off that day.

Max Clements was the editor of *Runway 26*, an aviation-oriented magazine. An intrepid Earhart researcher, Clements found documentation that suggested the time spent at Bandoeng was not entirely what most perceived it to be. Clements discovered that "a group of people was awaiting Earhart's arrival at Surabaya. She flew them to Bandoeng where, under the supervision of F. O. Furman, they installed superchargers on the Electra's engines."

The Navy seaplane tender *Swan* arrived at the assigned guard station in the Pacific. The U.S. Navy tug *Ontario* arrived at a point halfway between Lae, New Guinea, and Howland Island the previous evening. This now made three U.S. military vessels stationed in the Pacific awaiting word on the progress of Earhart's flight.

Earhart and Noonan took off just before noon from Bandoeng, Saturday, June 26. They were five days behind schedule. As the Electra approached the airport at Surabaya, Earhart checked to make certain all of the instruments were working properly. They were. They landed at 2:30 p.m. and made plans to depart early in the morning.

Around dawn of the next day, Sunday, June 27, they took off and headed for Koepang, on the western end of the island of Timor. They touched down at 1:30 p.m. local time. Their flight had been slowed because of strong headwinds. At Koepang, she informed airport officials that she would be there only long enough to refuel and wanted to depart as soon as possible for Darwin, Australia. As a result of a forecast of even stronger headwinds, Earhart and Noonan decided to remain in Koepang for the night. The following morning they lifted off at 6:30 a.m.

At 11:26 a.m. Darwin time, they landed and parked near the entrance to the administration building. There, the public health inspector found Earhart's vaccination certification was not in order. Since the Electra had recently traveled through and landed at locations where diphtheria, cholera, malaria, smallpox, and yellow fever were major problems, the inspector was concerned. He provided permission for Earhart and Noonan to proceed to the Hotel Victoria, where they had plans to stay the night, but insisted that they report to him any symptoms that might occur. In the meantime, he said, he would contact the Australian director general of health regarding the improper certification related to Earhart's vaccinations and inform them later of the decision.

Later, Earhart reported that her receiver had not worked properly since she left the United States and that the left landing gear shock absorber strut was low. When a technician examined the Bendix receiver, he discovered a burned-out fuse that he replaced. A short time later, the public health inspector contacted Earhart and Noonan at their hotel and informed them that exemptions had been granted for their vaccination certifications.

The following morning, June 29, Earhart lifted off at 6:49 a.m. The next destination was Lae, on the eastern end of the island of New Guinea. From Lae, Earhart and Noonan would commence their journey across a portion of the Pacific Ocean to Howland Island, by far the longest leg of the trip.

During the flight, Earhart noted that the Cambridge exhaust analyzer was inoperative once again. In addition, the carburetor air temperature gauges were not working, and the Sperry gyro horizon instrument relating to keeping the plane level was not functioning properly. During the flight, either Earhart did not make a significant number of transmissions, or her transmissions were not received by most of the stations. She and Noonan landed after flying for seven hours and forty-three minutes, at 3:02 p.m. Lae time.

At Lae, Earhart provided the mechanics with a list of five Electra malfunctions that needed fixing in addition to the exhaust analyzer. Since Earhart and Noonan were now facing the longest flight of their journey— a portion of the western Pacific Ocean over open water—it was imperative that all of the Electra's instruments and mechanical apparatuses be functioning properly.

· 17 ·

Final Preparations

$\mathcal{S}$hortly after arriving at Lae and clearing customs and health inspectors, Earhart met with Harry Balfour, who operated the airport radio station. Balfour handed Earhart a number of messages that had been waiting for her. Among them was one from the *Itasca* that was a review of the communication specifications. Earhart informed Balfour that her transmitter operated only on 3,105 and 6,210 kilocycles.

Earhart and Noonan went to the Hotel Cecil a short distance from the airport and checked in. Earhart was invited to dinner at the home of Eric H. Chater, the general manager of the airport. After she departed, Noonan went to the hotel bar and had a drink with James Collopy and Bertie Heath. Collopy was the district superintendent of the Australian civil aviation agency. Heath was a pilot. The three men regaled each other with their flying adventures as they drank. It was reported that Noonan became quite drunk.

It was around midnight when Noonan decided it was time to go to bed. Because he was staggering, Collopy assisted him to his room. Once there, Noonan got tangled up in the bed's mosquito netting and thrashed around, making a good deal of noise. Earhart, who was sleeping in an adjacent room, was awakened. She tried to communicate with Noonan through the thin walls, but he was too inebriated to understand anything.

On Wednesday morning, June 30, Earhart went to the radio station to check for messages and review the weather forecast. She told Balfour she would like to depart around noon. Forecasts had not yet arrived. Earhart proceeded to the hangar where the Electra was being worked on to determine whether it would be ready by noon. A mechanic informed her that an air scoop between two cylinders on the port engine required repair and that a takeoff would be unlikely until the next day.

58

Earhart sent a telegram to Putnam in Oakland. It read in part, "Radio misunderstanding and personnel unfitness probably will hold one day." This somewhat cryptic message has puzzled Earhart researchers over the decades. Some suggest her mention of "personnel unfitness" was a reference to Noonan and his drinking problem. Her reference to "radio misunderstanding" is not clear. Was she referring to a misunderstanding between her and the *Itasca*? Or did she mean she was having trouble understanding the radio operations procedure? No one knows.

By now Earhart and Noonan had been in Lae for eighteen hours and had received no flight forecasts. During another visit with Balfour, Earhart mentioned she was getting a lot of static on her radio receiver. Balfour went to inspect the system. He found that everything checked out properly. The likelihood is great that Earhart did not know how to operate the unit properly.

That evening, the mechanics had finished working on the Electra and deemed it ready. The plane was pushed out onto the field. Earhart started the engines and ran through the preflight routine. She discovered that the fuel pressure in the right engine was too low. The mechanics removed the fuel pump, a brand new one they had just installed. They rebuilt the old fuel pump and reinstalled it, and Earhart determined that it was working.

As Earhart was making plans to depart Lae in the morning, Noonan was attempting to calibrate his chronometer but having difficulties. The two undertook preparations for a 9:30 a.m. liftoff the next day. Earhart made arrangements for a thorough refueling.

Earhart returned to the hotel to await messages and the weather forecast. Noonan went to the hotel restaurant where he encountered Collopy, who invited him to have a drink. He informed Collopy that he had had enough the previous night to last him for a while. A few minutes later, Earhart came into the restaurant and joined the two men. She asked Collopy about wind conditions in the morning relative to her liftoff, and he explained the pattern. Noonan commented that he had been unable to manage a calibration on his chronometer. Earhart informed Noonan that they would make a test flight in the morning.

According to author Vincent Loomis, Earhart and Noonan agreed to retire early since they had an early morning takeoff. Noonan, however, decided to spend the night with his new friends, making it back to his hotel room only forty-five minutes before Earhart was knocking on his door to alert him that they would be leaving in two hours. Loomis referred to statements by Noonan's drinking partners that the navigator complained about Earhart's "strenuous pace."

At 6:00 a.m. on July 1, Earhart and Noonan went to the radio station. Balfour was already there and handed her several messages. One of them was a flight forecast that had emanated from Hawaii. According to the information, they would be facing headwinds of less than twelve miles per hour.

Noonan looked tired and peaked, and researchers claim he was feeling the effects of a hangover. At least one eyewitness maintained that Noonan was sober prior to takeoff, but the same eyewitness also confessed to having at least one drink with Noonan the previous evening. It was reported that when Noonan showed up that morning he told Earhart that he had a bit of a hangover. She was reputed to have called her navigator a "naughty boy." Collopy later stated that Noonan got only one hour of sleep before taking off from Lae.

At 6:35 a.m. on Thursday morning, July 1, Earhart started up the Electra for a test flight. She checked the radio transmitter, called the Lae station on 6,210 kilocycles, and satisfied with the results of the tests, lifted off at 7:05. She noted that the exhaust analyzer was functioning, as was the Sperry gyro. All of the other problems had apparently been taken care of.

After landing, the Electra was fueled to the maximum for the 2,556-mile flight to Howland Island. Earhart and Noonan expected to be in the air for eighteen hours. Because of the full complement of fuel they were carrying, Earhart deemed it necessary to reduce the weight of the Electra by removing all nonessential items to lighten the load. These included smoke bombs, flares, tools, spare parts, books, clothes, suitcases, and a number of personal belongings. They gave most of the items to several Lae residents.

Earhart went to the radio station and gave Balfour a number of charts and other items she did not feel were important enough to keep. A more recent forecast informed her of headwinds now predicted at a bit less than fifteen miles per hour. Noonan was finally able to get an accurate time check from a nearby station and found that his chronometer was three seconds slow.

Later, Balfour commented that he found it hard to believe that a flight such as this was to be undertaken "with so little regard for proper use of the radio and with an incapacitated navigator."

· 18 ·

From New Guinea to the Rising Sun

$\mathcal{A}$ few minutes before 10:00 a.m., Lae, New Guinea, time on July 2, 1937, Amelia Earhart, accompanied by Fred Noonan in his specially constructed compartment located several feet behind the cockpit of the Electra, taxied from the hangar toward the relatively short runway, only 3,000 feet long. The aircraft's carrying capacity was stressed with 1,100 gallons of fuel that should see them through the nineteen-hour flight to Howland Island, the next scheduled stop. It was the Electra's heaviest load since the beginning of the trip. Earhart researchers and experienced flyers have commented that the Electra was nearly 50 percent overloaded at the time of takeoff. At Howland, Earhart would refuel from tanks of gasoline that had been stored there for that purpose by the U.S. Navy.

Prior to boarding the Electra, Earhart cabled the U.S. Navy's auxiliary tug *Ontario* to send a series of Morse code *N*'s at ten minutes past each hour on 400 kilocycles so that she could take radio bearings on the ship with her radio direction finder when she was in the area. She never received a signal, but it remains unclear whether or not she listened in on the Bendix at all.

The Electra assumed a position in the northwest corner of the grass field. Earhart pointed the nose of the plane toward the southwest and the far end of the strip in order to take advantage of a light wind blowing from the ocean. The strip terminated at the edge of a bluff that rose nearly vertically from the shoreline. Beyond lay the shark-filled waters of the Pacific Ocean.

Earhart checked the instrument panel and revved up each engine. Satisfied that everything was in working order, she levered the engine throttles full forward and released the brakes. The Electra accelerated down the runway. A smoke bomb had been placed at the halfway point for reference.

The Electra was moving at just over sixty miles per hour as it passed. From this point on there was no backing off; the plane needed to lift off the runway or suffer the potential consequences of falling to the rocky shore at the bottom of the bluff.

At 10:00 a.m., July 2, the Electra took off from the Lae airfield. They had only three more scheduled stops to complete the flight around the world: Howland Island, Honolulu, and Oakland. Nearing the end of the runway, the wheels rose a few inches off the turf. The takeoff time was logged at 0000 Greenwich Civil Time (GCT).

The plane was off the ground, but the speed was too slow for an optimum climb. As the Electra passed the edge of the bluff, Earhart allowed the plane to drop gradually until it was only six feet from the surface of the ocean. The landing gear was retracting, and once the wheels were secured in the nacelles, some amount of the drag was reduced. Earhart worked the controls, and the airspeed gradually increased. The plane climbed slowly. When it was at least two hundred feet in the air, Earhart oriented the craft to a 073 heading on a direct line for Howland Island. Gradually the plane rose to a cruising altitude of four thousand feet. According to Noonan's calculations, they would arrive at their destination at daybreak the following morning. Noonan would be employing celestial navigation, that is, taking sightings on the stars until such time as they arrived at Howland Island.

After the Electra was out of sight, Balfour received a new forecast, one that included an update on the headwinds. Instead of the less than fifteen miles per hour that had been communicated earlier, the new forecast called for winds of 26.5 miles per hour. This would alter the Electra's flight time from eighteen hours to nineteen.

When the Electra was finally in the air and well on its way across the wide expanse of Pacific Ocean, the radioman at the Lae airfield radioed the U.S. Coast Guard cutter *Itasca* that everything was on schedule. The *Itasca* was holding a position just off Howland Island. Its responsibility was to provide communications, radio direction finding, and weather reports to Earhart. The crew of the vessel would also assist Earhart and Noonan with the refueling and maintenance. Further, the captain of the *Itasca* would keep all other stations apprised of Earhart's progress. Another ship, the U.S. Navy tug *Ontario*, was holding a position halfway between Lae and Howland Island. The responsibility of the *Ontario* was to make weather observations and provide reports as well as transmit radio homing signals for Earhart.

The Electra faced headwinds somewhat stronger than originally anticipated. Given the headwinds and the 157 miles per hour optimum true airspeed, Noonan calculated a ground speed of 142 miles per hour. Everything was still on schedule.

Before leaving Lae, Earhart made arrangements to transmit at eighteen minutes past each hour and to listen for messages from Lae at twenty minutes past each hour. Harry Balfour, the radio operator at Lae, provided reports of the stronger-than-expected and gradually increasing headwinds at 10:20, 11:20, and 12:20 local time, but Earhart never acknowledged him. The only response heard from Earhart was received at 0418 GCT (2:18 local time). Earhart, using the daytime frequency of 6,210 kilocycles, reported, "Height 7,000 feet, speed 140 knots." Because of what was determined to be local interference, much of the rest of her message could not be understood, though a reference to Lae was heard as well as the comment, "Everything OK." Earhart also transmitted that she had increased her air speed to 161 miles per hour in order to compensate for the stronger headwinds. Her next transmission was at 0519 GCT: "Height 10,000 feet. Position 150.7 east, 7.3 south. Cumulus clouds. Everything OK."

According to experienced pilots, maximum altitude for optimum fuel efficiency in the equatorial regions is two thousand feet below the recommended pressure altitude. It is presumed that, because of the presence of cumulus clouds (potential storm clouds), Earhart lifted the Electra to ten thousand feet in order to pass over the strong updrafts and eddies associated with the storm. The weight of the plane at this altitude would thus force Earhart to burn a significant amount of fuel to climb to and cruise at that altitude. The inefficiency related to fuel consumption could have a potential impact during the latter stages of the flight.

The position reported by Earhart placed her less than 220 statute miles from Lae and just over 450 miles from where they should have been assuming the original schedule had been maintained.

Earhart's 0618 GCT report did not arrive at Lae. The next transmission was at 0718 on 6,210 kilocycles: "Position 4.33 south, 159.7 east, height 8,000 feet over cumulus clouds. Wind 23 knots." This position was 850 miles from Lae, and they remained on a straight course for Howland Island. According to a variety of analyses of Earhart's transmissions in the years since her flight, it has been determined that her reported position at 0718 GCT was not where they were. In fact, given the schedule the Electra was maintaining, it was a position they would have been in one hour earlier. Earhart's transmission signals on 6,210 kilocycles had been strong both before and after her 0618 report. A handful of analysts have suggested that there was a delay between the time she sent the transmission and the time it was received by Balfour at Lae. Others have suggested that Noonan's position calculations were in error. Both explanations stretch the bounds of credulity. The truth is, a satisfactory explanation for the discrepancies in reporting and receiving time remains elusive to this day.

Given the headwinds along with the increased speed necessary to deal with them, the Electra would have just barely enough gasoline to get them to Howland Island. Having passed the worst of the cumulus cloud buildup, Earhart dropped to an altitude of eight thousand feet. This was still too high for optimum fuel efficiency.

Nothing was heard from either Balfour or the *Itasca* by Earhart during her scheduled 0815 GCT transmission on 3,105 kilocycles. It can be presumed that at 0910 GCT, Earhart listened for the *N*'s that were to be broadcast on 400 kilocycles. The log of the *Ontario* never showed that the *N*'s had been sent at that time or ever. At 1500 GCT, the tug, running low on fuel, set a course for American Samoa.

By 1000 GCT, the Electra was more than halfway to Howland Island. They were now past the point of no return. To turn around and head back to Lae would now be just as risky as continuing on to Howland Island, if not more so. They were now flying in the dark.

At around 1030 GCT, Earhart spotted some lights on the water. She reported "a ship in sight ahead." The ship was the SS *Myrtlebank* out of Auckland, New Zealand, and commanded by Captain Cort J. Holbrook. The position of the *Myrtlebank* at the time was eighty miles south of Nauru Island, for which it was bound. The officer in charge of the radio station at Nauru Island, Harold J. Barnes, logged in Earhart's message and responded over the island's 3,105 kilocycle radio. The *Itasca* heard the transmission, but if Earhart did, she did not respond.

By the time the Electra reached the *Myrtlebank*, it had traveled 1,414 statute miles in a period of ten and one-half hours. Howland Island still lay 1,142 statute miles away with an estimated flying time of eight and one-half hours. The revised estimated arrival time would be 1900 GCT.

At 1415 GCT, Earhart was nearing the Gilbert Islands. She transmitted her message at fifteen minutes past the hour on 3,105 kilocycles. The earlier strong headwinds had taken a toll on the fuel supply, but with four hours to go before reaching Howland Island, the amount of remaining fuel should have been sufficient.

At 1515 GCT, Earhart transmitted: "Itasca from Earhart. Overcast. Will listen on hour and half-hour on 3,105." At 1623 GCT, she transmitted her report, stating that it was "partly cloudy." They were 354 miles from Howland Island.

Before long, Earhart and Noonan would be greeted by the morning sun. During these early days of navigation, it was common for a navigator to plot a sun line—a single line of position from the sun plotted on a chart at right angles to it. The sun line would, with a fair degree of accuracy, update their position along an east-west course, but it was not particularly helpful relative to providing information pertinent to their maintaining the intended course directly to the island or veering off to the north or south. Because Howland Island was so small, any slight deviation from the intended course could cause the Electra to fly past it without Earhart or Noonan seeing it.

The way to compensate for a problem such as this was for the navigator to make a decision about the maximum distance it was reasonable for the plane to be accidentally off course to the north or south. The navigational term for this is the "area of uncertainty." The navigator would make a choice to veer either north or south from the presumed direct course. When the sun line of position indicated that they had progressed eastward as far as Howland Island, the pilot would then turn in the appropriate direction (north or south, depending on which direction the navigator chose to veer from the main course), and then, theoretically, fly directly to the intended destination, in this case, Howland Island. Flying the extra off-course for miles would delay their arrival time to around 1912 GCT.

By 1715 GCT, the Electra was running on the last of the fuel supply—a wing tank that carried ninety-seven gallons. Both engines could run off of this tank. With a fuel consumption rate of twenty gallons per hour, they would be able to remain airborne for another two- to two-and-a-half hours.

At 1744 GCT, Earhart transmitted, "Want bearing on 3,105 kilocycles on hour. Will whistle in mic." After pausing a moment, she continued, "About two hundred miles out, approximately." A few seconds of whistling followed, and she closed with the single word, "Northwest." The sun was now coming up.

At 1815 GCT, Earhart broadcast, "Please take bearing on us and report in half-hour. I will make noise in microphone. About one hundred miles out." Noonan plotted the sun line that ran 157–337 degrees across their course. At approximately 1833 GCT, the Electra was around sixty-five miles from its destination. Earhart began her descent, for it was imperative they get below the cloud line in order to be able to spot the island. At around one thousand feet, they were below the cloud base.

Presuming they were following Noonan's plan, Earhart would have turned north or south toward Howland Island around 1902 GCT, following the 157–337 sun line. The island should only be about fifteen to twenty miles away. It can also be presumed that because of the low angle of the sun, the pilot and navigator had to deal with a significant amount of glare coming off the ocean surface.

At 1912, Earhart sent her scheduled transmission on 3,105 kilocycles: "KHAQQ calling *Itasca*. We must be on you but cannot see you. But gas running low. Been unable to reach you by radio. We are flying at altitude of one thousand feet." By prearrangement, when the Electra got close to the island, the *Itasca* would release an abundant column of smoke. Since they were positioned just off Howland, the island would therefore be easier to spot. It has been estimated that such smoke could be seen from forty miles away and more.

The truth is, Earhart was nowhere near the *Itasca*. Based on an analysis of the radio logs by Paul Rafford as well as a study of the radio transmitting characteristics of Earhart's Electra, it was determined that she was 150 miles north-northwest of Howland Island when she made the above transmission.

By 1928 GCT, the Electra would have been flying along the 157–337 sun line for about forty miles. Earhart and Noonan could see neither the island nor the smoke from the *Itasca*. By this time, assuming the sun line course, they would have flown past the island.

Two minutes before the *Itasca*'s scheduled broadcast time (1928 GCT), Earhart transmitted on 3,105 kilocycles: "KHAQQ calling Itasca. We are circling but cannot hear you. Go ahead on 7,500 either now or on the scheduled time on half-hour." After receiving some Morse code signals, Earhart transmitted again at 1930 GCT: "KHAQQ calling Itasca. We received your signals but unable to get a minimum. Please take bearing on us and answer 3,105 with voice." Following this, she sent a series of long dashes in the hope that the ship could get a bearing on her. By this time, the Electra had only one-quarter tank of fuel remaining. This would give them thirty-five to forty minutes of flying time left.

At 2013 GCT, Earhart, speaking rapidly, transmitted on 3105: "We are on the line of position 157–337. Will repeat this message. We will repeat this message on 6,210 kilocycles. We are running north and south."

This was the last broadcast any of the designated stations ever picked up from Earhart. She was gone, and the immediate determination by United States Navy and Coast Guard, backed by U.S. government officials, was that the Electra crashed into the ocean somewhere near Howland Island, thus generating one of the greatest mysteries in history.

Over the next few days, newspapers across the world sported headlines relating to Earhart's and Noonan's disappearance, that they crashed and sank into the Pacific Ocean. Americans as well as others remained riveted to their radios and read newspapers as they followed the progress of the search for the missing aviatrix and her navigator.

· 19 ·

Flight Questions

$\mathcal{N}$umerous questions were subsequently raised relative to Earhart's flight that have yet to be answered adequately. For one, why were Earhart and Noonan unable to see the dense column of smoke emitted by the *Itasca* at a time when the ship's radio operators were convinced she was close to the vessel, if not directly overhead? It has been reported that similar plumes of smoke were able to be seen for great distances with little difficulty, and such a measure was used effectively numerous times in the past. Such a plume would have been impossible to miss. The answer may lie in the notion that Earhart and Noonan were nowhere near the *Itasca*. Subsequent research is strongly suggestive of the possibility that the Electra was in the area of the Marshall Islands over eight hundred miles to the northwest.

Related to the above, why was Noonan's navigation presumed to be so far off that they were unable to find Howland Island? Up to the point of arriving near their designated destination, as many believe they did, Noonan's navigating skills had served them well on the journey. It must be pointed out that he navigated them across the vast expanse of the Atlantic Ocean and the Sahara Desert only days earlier with little to no difficulty. Noonan had successfully navigated more than a dozen flights to Wake Island during his days with Pan American Airways. Wake Island was not much bigger than Howland. It should have been a simple task to locate the island.

Why couldn't Earhart get a minimum with her Bendix direction finder? It is an established fact that Earhart was less than competent and relatively uncooperative when it came to utilizing specialized radio equipment. Fred Noonan, however, was not only an accomplished and competent navigator, he knew his way around such communication devices and could have transmitted and received information easily. There is no evidence that any of the radio equipment was faulty. A possible answer may lie in the notion that Earhart, assuming she was on a clandestine aerial survey mission for the U.S. government, did not want her precise location identified.

Why couldn't Earhart hear the transmissions from the *Itasca* on 3,105 kilocycles? The fact that she did not respond to such transmissions is neither proof nor evidence that she did not hear them. If she was purposely off course relative to her aforementioned and hypothesized mission, she may very well have chosen to ignore such messages.

Another curious aspect of the series of events and circumstances involving this particular leg of the Earhart flight is related to the fact that the logs of the *Itasca* for this time period were classified "secret" for twenty-five years before being released on July 2, 1962. Those who have examined the logs have pointed out that (1) a great deal of confusion was manifest and (2) they appeared to have been tampered with. What is also apparent is that Warner K. Thompson, the *Itasca*'s commander, had no inkling of what his mission was. He was ordered to Howland Island from Honolulu. He presumed his responsibility was to assist Earhart, thus he had to radio division headquarters at San Francisco to provide him with her radio frequencies, schedules, and plans. Division headquarters reported back that they did not know. They informed Thompson that they heard a rumor that she might be using 6,210 kilocycles at fifteen minutes before the hour and fifteen minutes after in order to take bearings.

Most "authorized" inquiries, those supported by the U.S. government, into the disappearance of Amelia Earhart and Fred Noonan have been constructed around the belief that the Electra was close to Howland Island but ran out of fuel and crashed into the Pacific Ocean. Given that Earhart was on a special mission for the U.S. government, several alternative theories have been given attention over the decades following the disappearance. The more researchers and others among the curious have looked into what was being described as a mysterious disappearance, the more questions were raised. Among them were several related to the destination of record— Howland Island.

· 20 ·

The Mystery of Howland Island

$\mathcal{H}$owland Island is a tiny landmass in the vast expanse of the Pacific Ocean and is located 850 miles southeast of the Marshall Islands, slightly north of the equator, and 1,900 miles southwest of Honolulu. It is two miles long and perhaps a half mile wide, and it rises only a few feet above sea level. During the nineteenth century, when whaling was active in that part of the Pacific and when navigation was less sophisticated, ships often missed the island.

Many have wondered why Earhart and Noonan elected to land and refuel on such a tiny speck of land in the middle of the ocean, assuming it was their decision at all. The rationale for selecting this location may have come entirely from officials of the U.S. government.

Within a reasonable distance of Howland Island was Canton Island in the Phoenix group. This entire cluster of small islands in this remote section of the Pacific Ocean, unlike Howland Island, could have been spotted with no trouble at all. Furthermore, Canton Island boasted a long and well-maintained landing strip, one that had been recently constructed by Pan American Airways.

It must also be asked: If Howland was the predetermined destination for Earhart and Noonan, then why did the USS *Swan*, on learning of the downed pilots, head immediately to Canton Island? Why was a search party sent ashore on Canton Island a short time later and not Howland Island? It should also be mentioned that another search vessel, the USS *Colorado*, directed its search toward the Phoenix group, specifically Canton Island.

If, as the U.S. government maintained, Earhart and Noonan went down in the ocean somewhere near Howland Island, why then did they bother themselves with searching locations that did not fit with their contention and their subsequent press releases? Were they aware that the Electra did not, in fact, go into the ocean where they claimed and were now involved in a panic search to recover the aircraft that had clearly been fitted with spy cameras before it was found by another government?

In 1822, the captain of a whaling vessel out of Nantucket named the little isle after himself, but Worth Island was known only to a few and largely ignored as hardly anyone visited the insignificant feature. In 1842, another whaling captain named Howland renamed it after himself. By this time, the area—known as part of the South Seas whale fishery region—was encountered more often by whaling vessels, and the name stuck.

A survey conducted in the early 1930s concluded that Jarvis Island held the best potential for an airfield. Jarvis Island was located three hundred miles east of Howland Island. On May 13, 1936, Roosevelt gave jurisdiction of Howland Island to the secretary of the interior. In November 1936 a cable was sent to Interior Department official Richard B. Black instructing him to construct a landing field at Jarvis Island.

On December 7, 1936, Black received notice from Washington to scrap the Jarvis Island plan and advised him that the proposed airfield was to be constructed on Howland Island. (It has been suggested by some researchers that the distance between Lae, New Guinea, and Jarvis Island exceeded the fuel capacity of Earhart's Electra.) Because of governmental bureaucracy and weather delays, the construction of the airfield was not undertaken until February 5, 1937. The east-west landing strip was completed on March 4.

Until the construction activity was begun, Howland Island was unoccupied and rarely visited. In 1935, President Franklin D. Roosevelt, via the Bureau of Air Commerce, established an American presence on Howland, Jarvis, and Baker Islands in the Pacific. Roosevelt stated that they were to be colonized as the "American Equatorial Islands." To that end, he initiated an order for a party of young men to establish a temporary colony on the island. This was accomplished during the spring of 1935. The group consisted of six Hawaiian and Chinese American youths (some accounts say four). They were graduates of the Kamehameha School for Boys of Honolulu, a private educational institution. The tiny community was named Itascatown. The name came from the Navy ship that carried these first residents to the island and subsequently delivered supplies and provisions. The colonizers shared their habitat with tens of thousands of seabirds, hermit crabs, and rats. Their assignment was to live on the island and construct landing strips for aircraft.

Using equipment provided by the U.S. Navy, the colonists bladed out three 150-foot-wide intersecting runways onto the surface of Howland Island. The landing strips ranged from 2,400 feet to 4,000 feet. The building of these airstrips was undertaken with the utmost secrecy and urgency. The system of runways was named Kamakaiwi Field.

Though Roosevelt had earlier given jurisdiction of Howland Island to the secretary of the interior, he eventually turned the responsibility of overseeing the construction of the airstrips to the Public Works Administration. Later, during World War II, the Japanese conducted an air attack on Howland Island, killing two of the colonists. A short time later, the survivors were evacuated.

Howland Island was indeed a strange choice as a stop for Earhart and Noonan. There is no source of fresh water on the island; any fresh water available to the pilots, or anyone else, would have to be supplied from elsewhere, that is, delivered by ship.

Military personnel occasionally posted at Howland Island to operate and maintain radios and direction-finder equipment reported on the tens of thousands of birds found there. The bird population consisted of frigates, albatrosses, boobies, and terns. The frigates and boobies were described as being the size of buzzards. The bird population was estimated to be thirty thousand to forty thousand or more.

This large population of birds on an island as small as Howland presented a significant problem for airplanes landing and taking off. Bird populations in much smaller numbers have created similar difficulties for takeoffs and landings elsewhere and have been responsible for a number of airplane crashes. Determining that this could be a significant problem, and before attempting any landings and takeoffs from Howland Island, the U.S. military attempted to disperse the birds using dynamite and machine guns, all to no avail.

Reputable and experienced pilots who are familiar with the considerable hazards of large bird populations near airfields have suggested that Howland Island was never intended as a destination for Earhart and Noonan, that it may have been set up as a diversion from the original plan. Given the proximity of Gardner Island a short distance to the south, an island with a proven landing strip, fresh water, and minimal interference from birds, as well as nearby Canton Island, one is left wondering why Howland Island was considered at all.

One must wonder, therefore, why landing strips were constructed on this seldom-used island. The strips did not exist until a short time prior to the beginning of Earhart's proposed around-the-world flight. Eugene Vidal, then director of the Bureau of Air Commerce, a West Point graduate and a military flyer, was behind the construction of the airfield. Moreover, existing evidence reveals that, despite the presence of the landing strips, no aircraft ever landed there. All supplies were transported to the island by boat.

There is also some evidence that the geographical location of Howland Island had never been plotted accurately, and Earhart and Noonan quite possibly possessed locational information that was in error.

The question remains: Why was Howland Island publicized as a destination for Amelia Earhart? Could it have been a red herring? The selection of Howland Island represents another in a growing array of mysteries related to Earhart's around-the-world flight. There would be many more.

· 21 ·

The Flight Path

$\mathcal{P}$aul Rafford Jr. worked with the U.S. space program during the 1960s and 1970s as a communications expert as well as an astronaut recovery specialist. Prior to World War II, Rafford had been a radio operator for Pan American Airways. During the 1960s, Rafford grew fascinated with the Amelia Earhart disappearance and spent much of his spare time researching and studying the multiple aspects of it. Aware of the skills of Fred Noonan as a navigator as well as the degree of skills possessed by the aviatrix, Rafford developed an intense curiosity relative to how the two could have possibly become lost.

Over time, Rafford obtained documents pertaining to the Earhart flight and disappearance, among them the official report filed by Jim Collopy. Collopy's account indicates that, based on his in-person observations regarding the preparation for the departure from Lae, New Guinea, Earhart "should have had several hours worth [of fuel] left when the *Itasca*'s radiomen last heard her voice, even though she thought she was running low."

A historian named Dr. Francis X. Holbrook likewise accumulated a number of Earhart-related documents, including copies of radio message traffic as preparations were being made to depart Lae. Further, Holbrook interviewed a number of people who had heard Earhart's transmissions after leaving Lae. Holbrook located Harry Balfour, the Guinea Airways radio operator who was with Earhart and Noonan on the day of the Lae departure and who communicated with the aviatrix during the first eight hours of her flight. He also located and interviewed T. H. Cude, who was director of police on Nauru Island in 1937. Cude maintained that he had heard Earhart's transmissions as she approached Nauru, stating that she could see the lights on the island.

73

As Rafford pored over the documents and related materials, a curious fact emerged: Earhart had not followed the established and publicized direct route from Lae to Howland Island. With assistance from Balfour, claims Rafford, Earhart flew near Nauru Island, which was not located along the publicized route. Subsequent research by Rafford and others confirmed this to be the case. Employing information gleaned from correspondence between Balfour and Holbrook and applying information taken from interviews, Rafford was able to piece together what he claims was the actual last flight of Amelia Earhart.

Rafford learned that because of Fred Noonan's problem with alcohol, he was not in a position to provide reliable help with the navigation. In fact, he claims, Earhart attempted to convince Balfour to take Noonan's place during this last section of the flight. Balfour considered it but declined because of "a feeling of impending doom."

Balfour arranged Earhart's departure time such that she would arrive over a visual navigation fix he had chosen for her—the Nukumanu Islands, 750 miles east of Lae. From there she would travel to Nauru Island. On approaching Nauru, Earhart would be able to see the array of lights at the large phosphate mining operation there. After spotting the lights, she could orient her course toward Nauru. After Nauru, there would be no checkpoints to guide her toward Howland Island.

Between 10:30 and 11:30 GMT, Nauru Islanders sitting near their radios heard Earhart's transmissions. When interviewed years later, they claimed that the aviatrix called several times, stating that she could see the lights of the island. At this point, she still had more than 1,100 miles to go to reach Howland Island.

Unable to locate Howland Island, according to author Loomis, Earhart had no choice but to follow the contingency plans she developed prior to leaving the United States: turn around and fly back to the Gilbert Islands and land on a stretch of beach. Loomis, employing analysis and conclusions developed by Rafford and others, determined that Earhart, presuming her location to be near Howland Island, set out on a course she believed would take them to the Gilbert Islands. Since they were so far north, however, they were headed directly for the Marshall Islands.

Author James Donahue advances the notion that Earhart, after passing Nauru Island, purposely changed her course toward the northeast in order to make a pass over the Marshall Islands. Following that, he hypothesizes that her plan was to then head for Howland Island.

Author Joe Klaas offers yet another perspective on Earhart's flight path. Klaas was convinced that, as a result of the secret meetings with Bernard Baruch and General Westover, she could have flown the Electra on a photographic mission to the Truk Islands (today called Chuuk Lagoon), a major Japanese possession in the Pacific located about 1,200 miles northeast of New Guinea. With the "increased range and speed of the XC-35's now supercharged engines, she could then have flown directly to Canton Island, breaking radio silence only after intercepting her announced course a couple of hundred miles west of Howland Island so that the direction-finders, if they had worked, would finally pick her up in the right direction." On this course, according to Klaas, Earhart could have easily made photographs while passing over the Japanese airfields at Ponape, Kusaie, and Tarawa, all along a course toward Canton Island.

In support of Klaas's theory, Robert Myers, who had monitored radio transmissions on a ham radio set during Earhart's flight, reported that shortly after taking off from Lae, New Guinea, the aviatrix told Balfour that Noonan had handed her a sealed message. The message contained a set of instructions, according to Myers, ordering her to turn northeast toward Truk by way of the Admiralty Islands.

Myers's transcriptions of the communications between Earhart and Balfour have the aviatrix telling the radio operator: "They should have told you! They should have told you about this! I am not sure if I want to do this! It is different. Who am I going to talk to? Who is going to give me the radio reports?"

The tone of Earhart's message suggests that she had been kept in the dark regarding the actual route until that moment. During the transmissions, Earhart asked Balfour whether he had been aware of the secret instructions. He replied that he was not, that the only thing requested of him was to provide weather reports to her until she was four hundred miles from Lae.

The first person to advance the possibility that Earhart flew over Truk Atoll, as well as perhaps Kwajalein Atoll, was Captain George C. Carrington. Carrington published his findings in a book titled *Amelia Earhart: What Really Happened at Howland Island, Unabridged Report IV*. The publication contains a quantity of impressively researched material, including evidence of the participation of the U.S. government in the flight. Carrington, along with many others, argues that Earhart and Noonan came down in the Marshall Islands and were captured by the Japanese.

In 1983, a Freedom of Information Act–declassified O2 intelligence report revealed that, despite what was reported by the U.S. government, Amelia Earhart, on nearing Howland Island, transmitted a message stating that she was turning north. The O2 report stated that "Her signals became fainter as she continued to head north until they were no longer received." The Marshall Islands were northwest of Howland Island.

Additional significant discoveries of Earhart-related information by a man named Carroll F. Harris were reported by author David K. Bowman.

While on active duty with the U.S. Navy, Harris had been given an assignment to microfilm "highly sensitive files in the office of the Chief of Naval Operations." Harris was forbidden to take notes while pursuing the task, but he remembered that the Earhart file "took up three-quarters of a file drawer" and covered, among other things, "details of the precautions to keep Earhart's actual route from Lae to Howland [Island] secret. The files indicated that she was to take a different, longer flight path than her publicly announced one."

Thus, it becomes clearer with each passing year that Amelia Earhart's around-the-world flight was not entirely what the public assumed it was. It had far-reaching implications, all of which placed Earhart and Noonan in danger.

Elgen Long, a pilot and author, claimed he had "located" Earhart's Electra in 16,800 feet of water thirty-five miles west-northwest of Howland Island. Long arrived at this conclusion, he explained, "by examining the strengths and weaknesses of radio signals from the plane before it ditched, as reflected in logs kept by radio operators on ships in the area at the time." Contemporary radio experts insist Long's calculations cannot be taken seriously since radio transmission and reception, as well as determining distance and location, during that time was unreliable. In truth, Long located nothing, and there appears to be no substantive basis for his claims, which have amounted to nothing.

In 2002, a man named David Jourdan, owner of Nauticos Corporation, undertook a search for Earhart's Electra in the waters off Howland Island. He was unsuccessful but was apparently encouraged enough to try again in 2005. The second expedition, according to Jourdan, employed more updated sonar equipment. Jourdan also claimed he was in possession of accurate information relative to where the plane might be located, though he never explained what that information was or from where or whom he obtained it. Though the Nauticos Corporation website promised progress relative to the search, nothing was ever discovered. The search cost $1.5 million. At this writing, Nauticos has announced plans for yet another attempt at locating the Electra near Howland Island, but no one is holding his breath.

From time to time, an announcement is made relative to claims of a new "discovery" of all or part of Earhart's Electra. The claims are made, for the most part, based on underwater sonar images. Quite often, when an anomaly appears on the floor of the ocean near Howland Island and/or some of the other proposed locations where Earhart might have come down, someone feels compelled to make the claim that it is from the Electra. To date, none of these claims has been verified.

THE GARDNER ISLAND THEORY

This theory promotes the idea that Earhart, on missing Howland Island, chose to continue on toward Gardner Island (now Nikumaroro Island) to the south-southeast. The theory continues that, on arriving at Gardner Island, she made a shore landing. From here, according to some reports, she was able to continue broadcasting for several days until her batteries wore down. Then, according to another explanation, the Electra was subsequently blown from the shore into the nearby ocean as a result of a storm and sank out of sight. The theory continues that Earhart and Noonan, abandoned on the island, survived off of what rations they had in their possession until perishing or being picked up by the Japanese.

This theory was originated by members of an organization called The International Group for Historic Aircraft Recovery (TIGHAR). It is difficult to understand why this theory has endured with this organization or with anyone else, for that matter. As evidence for its position, this group offers the discovery of a size 9 shoe sole found on the island, a piece of sheet metal that appeared to come from some type of aircraft, and a navigator "bookcase."

This same organization reported in May 2012 the discovery of "an object resembling a twenty-two-foot-long airplane wing found off the coast of Gardner Island." Examination of the sonar image that was generated yields the only logical conclusion that the sea-bottom anomaly could be anything. To make the determination that it is an airplane wing represents a generous interpretation as well as a considerable leap of faith.

The truth is, none of the evidence associated with Gardner Island can in any way be logically connected to Earhart or Noonan with any certainty and could have originated from a multitude of sources. Despite a number of searches, not another single piece of any kind of pertinent evidence was ever found on the island. Furthermore, navy aircraft conducted two flyovers of Gardner Island during the extended search for the Electra. The island is relatively tiny; a plane such as the Electra would have been easy to spot if it had been there.

The evidence advanced by TIGHAR, along with the rationale that Earhart landed on Gardner Island, is at best spurious and easily rejected.

THE NEW BRITAIN ISLAND THEORY

A man named David Billings was with an Australian army patrol on New Britain Island in 1945. The patrol was deep in the island's jungle and fleeing a contingent of Japanese soldiers in pursuit. One morning, the Australians came upon the wreckage of a twin-engine plane. On examining it, one of the soldiers found a metal tag on an exposed engine mount. On the tag were two identification codes: C/N 1055 and S3H1. A notation of the find, along with the two numbers, was made on a map that was carried by another of the soldiers.

This evidence could be significant in that the C/N, or construction number, of Earhart's Electra was 1055. Additionally, the number S3H1 was the model of the Wasp engines that were allegedly installed in the Electra. Because the Japanese pursuit was closing in rapidly, the Australians had no time to inspect the plane further. A subsequent expedition was undertaken years later by one of the Australian soldiers in an attempt to relocate the plane, but it failed to do so.

The map on which the location of the plane was marked, along with the identification numbers, has been in the possession of the widow of one of the soldiers and has been displayed on the website of the man named David Billings. It is odd that, in the years that the map has been available, no one has ever relocated the alleged missing aircraft on New Britain Island, if in fact it was ever there in the first place.

A thorough analysis of the radio transmissions made by Earhart after departing Lae, New Guinea, provides no support whatsoever for this theory. The signal strength of her final transmission is enough evidence to prove she was nowhere near New Britain Island.

While the New Britain Island theory is provocative as a result of the numbers found on the exposed engine mount, it also carries with it a level of absurdity. The western tip of New Britain Island is only one hundred miles from Lae, New Guinea. Given that most researchers are convinced that, on the basis of abundant evidence, Earhart and Noonan were in the air for more than eighteen hours, then what could they have possibly been doing, and why and how would they have wound up so close to where they started out unless they turned around and tried to return to the Lae airport? Nothing relative to the New Britain Island theory holds up under logical scrutiny. Furthermore, despite the availability of a map that supporters contend shows the location of the downed aircraft on New Britain Island, it is baffling that no one has relocated it to date. Unless, of course, it was never there in the first place.

THE HULL ISLAND THEORY

Hull Island is located to the southeast of Howland Island. Advanced by British writer James Donahue, the theory that Earhart came down on or near this isle is based on his notion that postdisappearance radio signals attributed to Amelia Earhart were triangulated by Pan American Airways and determined to have come from Hull Island. Donahue, though passionate in his Hull Island hypothesis, provides no evidence whatsoever to verify the triangulation rationale. Furthermore, not a scintilla of evidence of a downed aircraft was ever found anywhere on or near Hull Island.

THE SYDNEY ISLAND THEORY

The most notable proponent of the Sydney Island Theory was Robert Myers, who as a boy hung around the Oakland airport during the time Earhart was preparing for her around-the-world flight and got to know her as well as Fred Noonan and others involved in the operation. Myers claimed to have listened to transmissions from Earhart on a ham radio set for several days that provided specifics relative to her plane coming down near Sydney Island, part of the Phoenix Island group, and being captured by the Japanese. Phoenix Island is approximately seven hundred miles southeast of Howland Island.

No credible evidence exists that Earhart came down on or near Sydney Island. Further, it is ludicrous to assume that, had Earhart been captured by the Japanese, they would have allowed her to continue to broadcast messages.

THE SAIPAN ISLAND THEORY

A handful of Earhart researchers suggest that the Electra came down on the island of Saipan, a Japanese possession in the Mariana Islands located about five hundred miles north-northeast of Guam. This theory is based on reports that the Electra, along with Earhart and Noonan, were seen on that island. The evidence for the presence of the aviatrix and her navigator, as well as the aircraft, on Saipan has been well documented and will be treated in a subsequent chapter. Though eventually arriving at Saipan, the Electra and its occupants did not come down on that island. Instead, they were transported there after being located and recovered at Mili Atoll.

THE MILI ATOLL THEORY

While the above theories carry with them little to no credible evidence and, in most cases, strain logic, the Mili Atoll theory differs from them in that numerous eyewitnesses reported the forced landing of an aircraft resembling the Electra at this cluster of coral and sand located at the southeasternmost atoll in the Marshall Islands group. So compelling are the eyewitness and other accounts that the Mili Atoll theory deserves close attention.

Amelia Earhart standing in front of an airplane propeller. Schlesinger Library, Radcliffe Institute, Harvard University, photograph by Frederick Bradley

Herbert Hoover presenting the National Geographic Society medal to Amelia
Earhart, with Dr. Gilbert Grosvenor at left, at the White House, Washington,
D.C., June 21, 1932. Library of Congress, Prints & Photographs Division,
photograph by Harris & Ewing LC-H2-B-5256

Amelia Earhart strapping on a parachute with the assistance of her husband, George Palmer Putnam, as she prepares for a cross-country autogyro flight, May 28, 1931. Schlesinger Library, Radcliffe Institute, Harvard University

Amelia Earhart checking over her plane with mechanics at Wheeler Field,
Honolulu, Hawaii. Schlesinger Library, Radcliffe Institute, Harvard University

Amelia Earhart and George Palmer Putnam mark the course to be followed by Earhart on her transpacific flight as the plane was being made ready at Burbank, California, 1935. Schlesinger Library, Radcliffe Institute, Harvard University

Amelia Earhart sitting atop her transpacific plane, caught by the camera at the Burbank, California, airport before her high-wing Lockheed was shipped by liner to the Hawaiian Islands, 1935. Schlesinger Library, Radcliffe Institute, Harvard University, photograph by Pan-Pacific Press Bureau photographer

Amelia Earhart with the managers of Guinea Airways and Fred Noonan, who is smoking. This photo was taken in Lae, Papua New Guinea, on June 30, 1937. Schlesinger Library, Radcliffe Institute, Harvard University

Amelia Earhart seated on the floor, looking at some charts in Honolulu, Hawaii, 1936.
Schlesinger Library, Radcliffe Institute, Harvard University

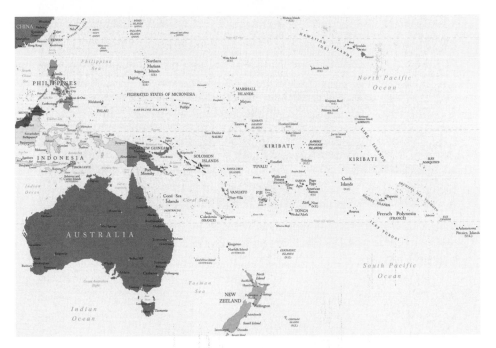

Map of Oceania. Thinkstock

Amelia Earhart standing on wall under wrought-iron lantern, overlooking
a valley in California, 1933. Schlesinger Library, Radcliffe Institute,
Harvard University

· 23 ·

Downed at Mili Atoll

$\mathcal{T}$he argument rages on among Earhart researchers to this day relative to what became of her: Did she crash and sink near Howland Island as the U.S. government proclaimed, or did she wind up coming down on or near an island or atoll where she was found and picked up by the Japanese? A related argument is devoted to the topic of whether or not Earhart was on a spy mission for the United States. Though the U.S. government denies such a thing, as one would expect it to, evidence points to the probability that the Electra had been fitted with sophisticated camera gear to be used for photographing Japanese military installations in the Pacific.

Regardless of one's position on such matters, there exist some truths that must be considered. Mili Atoll is the southeasternmost atoll in the Marshall Islands group and located some one thousand miles northwest of Howland Island. Atolls are composed mainly of coral that grew in the shallow waters around ancient volcanoes that have long since subsided below the surface of the ocean. As a result of sea level changes, portions of the semicircular coral reefs yield low-lying islands somewhat linear in nature.

When the Japanese occupied the Marshall Islands group, they constructed an airfield on Mili Island in the southwestern section of the group. On arriving, they installed a type of rule similar to what they inflicted on their other Pacific Island possessions. They replaced local governments with military law and established rice, sugar, and rubber plantations wherein the natives were forced to work for small pay. Docks, ports, and landing fields were constructed using the labor of the natives. If any workers complained, they were punished severely and sometimes even killed.

Jororo Alibar was a Marshall Islander who lived on one of the islands of Mili Atoll. Jororo, a fisherman, had rowed to Barre Island in the company of several friends. Barre Island is located along the northwestern edge of the atoll. Even though they were instructed by the Japanese officers to stay away from Barre Island, the fishermen, all in their teens, had gone ashore and were occupied with some task at the upper end of the beach near the forest when they heard the sound of an airplane. The Marshall Islanders had seen airplanes before when Japanese aircraft were flown over the atoll. This one, however, sounded as if it was losing altitude. The young fishermen began to make their way down to the beach to get a better view.

At least three theories have been advanced in efforts to explain why the Electra came down. One is that it was shot down, a theory bolstered by claims of Japanese pilots. Another is that it simply ran out of gas. This second theory is plausible, given the distance the Electra traveled from New Guinea. The third, one advanced by experienced pilot and dogged Earhart researcher Elgen Long, brings up the notion of the failure rate of components of the Electra. Long points out that after departing on her around-the-world flight, Earhart never flew the Electra for as long as ten hours without experiencing mechanical failures of one kind or another involving the propellers, the electrical system, the fuel system, or the exhaust analyzer. In addition to these, according to Long, there were five more "mechanical failures of a non-routine nature." Long thus provides the possibility of mechanical failure having a role in the downing of the Electra.

After a few steps the fishermen paused and watched as the silver airplane made a hard landing on an offshore reef. As they stared at the craft, two people exited from the middle and produced what Jororo referred to as "a yellow boat which grew." Clearly, this was an inflatable life raft. When the raft was filled with air, the two strangers climbed into it and paddled for the shore. Jororo and his companions, fearing that the newcomers were Japanese and would catch them on the island, retreated into the dense undergrowth found beyond the upper edge of the beach.

As they watched, the two newcomers arrived at the shore. One of them, carrying a metal case, walked to a nearby kanal tree and buried the case. At this point, the fishermen observed that the two strangers were not the Japanese they were accustomed to; their skin was white. These were the first Americans the native islanders had ever seen. It is worth pointing out here that while in Lae, Noonan had purchased a metal briefcase and was seen carrying it aboard the Electra prior to taking off for Howland Island.

At the sound of the descending airplane, the Japanese military stationed on Mili Island, located south-southwest of Barre Island, procured one of the local fishing boats, crossed the lagoon, and steered toward the downed aircraft. On seeing the two figures on the beach, they anchored the craft, waded ashore, and approached them. Jororo and his friends slunk deeper into the undergrowth, for they did not wish to be seen by the Japanese soldiers, who made life miserable for the islanders. If they were found on the island, it was possible they would be apprehended and punished, even killed.

As the small contingent of soldiers approached, the two figures on the beach stood and awaited their arrival. From the brush, Jororo could hear the soldiers loudly and animatedly hurling questions at the newcomers. The two from the airplane responded in a language the fishermen had never before heard. At one point, one of the soldiers slapped the shorter of the two Americans, who screamed in response. At that point, Jororo realized it was a woman.

Following a few minutes of futile attempt at dialog, the Japanese pushed the Americans down the beach and toward the location where the fishing boat was anchored. After forcing them into the boat, they departed toward the south-southwest for Mili Island. Jororo and his friends remained in hiding for a long time after the Japanese left.

Word of the capture of the two American flyers spread rapidly throughout Mili Atoll. Bosket Diklan, the native wife of a Japanese officer, learned that the presence of the Americans represented a problem for the occupying army. Bosket's husband was immediately called to Jaluit Island, due west of Mili Atoll. Before leaving, he impressed on her the importance of secrecy relative to the two American flyers.

Fuji Firmosa was a Japanese pilot stationed on the aircraft carrier *Kaga* in the Marshall Islands in 1937. Firmosa was one of several pilots who were alerted to the presence of Earhart's plane in Japanese airspace. After taking off from the *Kaga*, Firmosa encountered the Electra in the air and made two passes at it. During the second pass, he claimed he fired several rounds of bullets at the plane. Once struck, the plane began descending when Firmosa lost sight of it.

Based on eyewitness testimony, the Electra, in addition to being seen by the young fishermen on Barre Island, was spotted by a Japanese fishing boat. Following some radio transmissions to the military leaders from this boat, another Japanese ship was summoned and arrived nine or ten days after the landing of the Electra. The coal tender *Kosyu* possessed the facilities with which to salvage the Electra and transport it elsewhere.

Tomaki Mayazo worked on the *Kosyu*, which at the time lay empty in the harbor at Jaluit, one of the Marshall Islands, while waiting to take on cargo. Mayazo recalled to an interviewer years later that as he was preparing to load coal into the *Kosyu* one evening on July 9, 1937, a military officer pressured him to finish his job quickly as the ship had been dispatched to Mili Atoll to pick up an airplane and its two American pilots.

On July 10, the *Kosyu* arrived at Mili Island in the atoll. Earhart and Noonan were placed aboard the ship. The vessel then traveled to Barre Island where, with the assistance of heavy canvas slings and a crane, the Electra was loaded aboard and placed on the fantail of the ship. This done, the *Kosyu* steered back toward Jaluit, where it arrived seven to ten days after the Electra had come down on Barre Island.

On July 13, Japanese foreign minister Koki Hirota sent a message from Tokyo to Ambassador Yoshida in London. The message read: "The *Advertiser* here reports that they received a London International News dispatch at 2:00 a.m. today to the effect that a Japanese fishing vessel had rescued the Earhart plane. Please verify this and confirm by return."

The *Kosyu* arrived back at the island of Jaluit. John Heine, a grandson of German missionary Carl Heine, lived on Jaluit as a youth. He told Earhart investigator Bill Prymak that one day the schoolmaster took the students on a short trip to the harbor. When they arrived, stated Heine, "A ship had just pulled in and appeared to be towing a barge with an airplane on it." The plane, he said, was unlike any Japanese aircraft he had ever seen. He was later told it was an American plane and that a woman had been flying it when it crashed at Mili Atoll.

On the ship's arrival at Jaluit, the director of health services was summoned, as was a sixteen-year-old medical corpsman trainee named Bilimon Amran (sometimes spelled Amaran). The two were escorted aboard the *Kosyu*, and Amran was ordered to treat the wounds of the male flyer. On being admitted to the room in which the two prisoners were held under guard, Amran realized the two captives were Americans. The woman, he noted, wore trousers similar to what a man would wear, and her hair was cut short. The man, according to Amran, had blue eyes, something Amran had never seen before. Noonan's military records state his eyes were blue-gray.

Amran was ordered not to speak to the prisoners and to get busy treating the man's wounds. He had been cut on the head and had a serious four-inch-long gash on one knee. It was explained that the man had suffered the injury when the plane crash-landed on the reef at Mili Atoll. In the nearly two weeks that had elapsed, the wound had become infected and inflamed. Amron cleaned it, applied an ointment, and rebandaged it.

As Amran repacked his medical kit, he overheard the Japanese officers mention that the ship was going to leave Jaluit for Kwajalein and then proceed on to Roi-Namur, two islands in the Marshall group where the Japanese had military bases. From there, it would continue to Truk Atoll and then on to the island of Saipan. Amran also heard some of the officers refer to the female prisoner as "Ameera." Amran learned later that her name was Amelia.

Some of the crew members of the *Kosyu* told Amran that the man and woman had been picked up at Mili Atoll, where their plane had come down. A Japanese officer pointed toward the stern of the ship, where Amran saw an airplane that had been strapped down. Amran described the plane as silver, having two motors and a broken left wing. The plane was still wrapped in the stout canvas slings that had been used to retrieve it from the water. Finally, Amran was escorted off the vessel. The *Kosyu* departed Jaluit on July 19.

Bilimon Amran died in 1996. When interviewed about the incident aboard the *Kosyu*, he never wavered in his story. Amran was described by Jaluit residents as "one of the most respected, revered, and successful persons in the Marshall Islands." He was, in short, a credible eyewitness.

Eric de Bisschop, identified as a French explorer who was sailing across the Pacific toward the Hawaiian Islands, reported spotting Earhart and Noonan on Jaluit. For a time, de Bisschop was held prisoner by the Japanese. He said the two Americans were also prisoners.

Added to the above eyewitness accounts of the Electra coming down at Mili Atoll is a statement from the United Nations ambassador from the Republic of the Marshall Islands. On May 20, 2002, he stated, "She definitely landed in the Marshall Islands." He said that he personally had interviewed a number of islanders who saw Earhart after her landing and capture.

A Marshall Islander named Dr. John told interviewers in later years of seeing an aircraft "go down in the water about two hundred feet offshore on one of the islands." While he saw the plane, he was never close enough to observe the crew.

During the 1970s, author Vincent Loomis interviewed a number of Marshall Islanders relative to the Earhart disappearance. One of them was a woman who stated, "I tell you I saw this airplane and the woman pilot and the Japanese taking the woman and the man with her away." When asked where she saw the plane, the woman pointed and said "Over there . . . next to Barre Island. That's where it landed."

In 1978, Vincent Loomis traveled to the Marshall Islands to search for Earhart's plane, which, despite the information that the Japanese had retrieved it, he believed could still be found there. He had no luck locating the craft, but he interviewed a number of residents of Mili Atoll, among them two local senators. One, Amata Kabua, told Loomis that he, along with most of the residents of the atoll, were well aware that Amelia Earhart had gone down near Barre Island. Others interviewed by Loomis throughout the area told the same story.

Robert Reimers was born on Jabor in the Jaluit Atoll in 1909 and lived there for most of his life. Reimers was a successful businessman who owned hotels, travel agencies, shopping centers, and other businesses in Majuro. When interviewed by Earhart researcher Bill Prymak, he stated that Earhart's capture by the Japanese was widely known by everyone on the island, "that a Japanese fishing boat found Earhart, her navigator, and the airplane near

Mili Atoll. They were transferred to a bigger boat and brought to the harbor at Jabor, eight miles south of Emidj on Jaluit Atoll. There was no mystery. Everyone knew it."

Following the 1944 occupation of the Marshall Islands by U.S. servicemen, soldiers assigned there heard stories from the natives of a "white lady pilot and a white man" who had crash-landed at Mili Atoll and were taken prisoner by the Japanese. One marine described encountering a barracks room that had clearly been prepared to house a woman. Among the items found in the room was a suitcase that contained newspaper clippings about Amelia Earhart. Also found were a woman's clothing and a locked diary with the title "10-Year Diary of Amelia Earhart." What became of these articles after the war is unknown.

And there is this: Just before he passed away in 1966, U.S. Navy Fleet Admiral Chester Nimitz was quoted as saying, "Earhart and her navigator did go down in the Marshalls and were picked up by the Japanese." Nimitz, who controlled a great portion of the U.S. Navy and often rubbed elbows with the nation's leaders, would certainly have had access to critical and top secret information regarding the incident. Furthermore, Alfred Capelle, the United Nations ambassador to the Marshall Islands, told an Associated Press reporter in 2002 that "Amelia Earhart definitely came to the Marshall Islands in 1937."

Despite the official government position that Earhart crashed and sank near Howland Island, an increasing number of people were growing cognizant of the truth. Among them was Amelia's mother, Amy Otis Earhart. During an interview with the *New York Times*, Mrs. Earhart stated that she "knew" her daughter had ended up a prisoner of the Japanese. Twelve years after the aviatrix vanished, an interview with Earhart's mother was published in the *Los Angeles Times* on July 24, 1949. In part, the interview contained the following:

> I have kept quiet through the many years, but certainly this could hurt no one now. I am convinced she was on some sort of government mission, probably on verbal orders, she wouldn't tell me. I am equally sure she didn't make a forced landing on the open sea. She landed on a tiny atoll, one of the many in that general area of the Pacific and was picked up by a Japanese fishing boat and taken to the Marshall Islands, then under Japanese control. She was ordered taken to Japan. There she met with an accident, an arranged accident that ended her life.

What exactly did Amy Otis Earhart know, and how did she arrive at this knowledge? While parts of her interview may be in error, there is obvious consistency relative to the notion that her daughter survived her crash at or near the Marshall Islands.

Given the quantity and quality of the evidence, it has become increasingly clear that the Electra came down on Mili Atoll in the Marshall Islands. Controversy has surfaced as to whether the plane was shot down, forced down, or simply ran out of gas. Regardless of the reasons, there exists little in the way of compelling evidence to suggest that the Electra came down in any other location.

It is clear, then, that Amelia Earhart and Fred Noonan did not perish in a crash of the Electra, as was claimed by the government of the United States, and that they were alive for a significant amount of time after the U.S. officially assumed the position that she was dead and the case was closed.

Just how long did Earhart survive following the alleged crashing and sinking of the Electra? The accumulating evidence suggests that she remained a prisoner of the Japanese for eight years before she was found and rescued by the conquering armies following the end of World War II.

· 24 ·

The Search

$\mathcal{O}$n learning of the disappearance of Earhart and Noonan, the U.S. government immediately ordered an extensive search of the region. The U.S. Navy was placed in charge. The aircraft carrier *Lexington* arrived in the area of Howland Island on July 13. From the USS *Lexington*, the mightiest aircraft in the U.S. fleet, fighter planes were ordered to within seventy-five miles of the Gilbert Islands and to within 250 miles of the Marshall Islands. In all, the United States committed to the search one aircraft carrier, one battleship (the 33,000-ton USS *Colorado*), four destroyers, a cruiser, two Coast Guard cutters, a minesweeper, and sixty-five aircraft, as well as a number of other support vessels from the U.S. Navy and Coast Guard.

The search was hampered from the beginning. For one thing, the only maps available depicting the Pacific Ocean's islands and shoals in this region were compiled ninety-six years earlier by whaling companies and were woefully inaccurate. For nearly a week, planes flew seven hundred feet above the surface of the sea searching for evidence of the Electra. According to government documents, a total of 151,556 square miles were covered. The *Lexington*, along with three other vessels, covered another 22,640.

Oddly, in spite of the fact that the official position of the U.S. government was that the Electra came down in the area of Howland Island, the USS *Swan* was immediately dispatched to Canton Island to look for the plane. On arriving at the island, a large search party was sent onto the island to hunt for the wreckage of the Electra. The USS *Colorado* went straight to the Phoenix Island group.

The U.S. Navy communicated with the second secretary of the Japanese embassy, Tsuneo Hayama, that a clue derived from one of Earhart's messages suggested that she was near a point two hundred miles north of Howland

Island and that the USS *Lexington* and the *Colorado* were on their way to that location. They requested assistance from the Japanese. In truth, both vessels were on their way to the Phoenix group of islands located four hundred miles southeast of Howland Island. It remains unclear whether the U.S. Navy was providing false information to the Japanese or whether they were simply lost or confused.

On July 3, Karl Pierson, the chief engineer of the Patterson Radio Corporation in Los Angeles, California, was approached by officials from the Federal Bureau of Investigation and sworn to secrecy regarding any radio messages that might have been received from Earhart during her flight. Walter McMenamy, a Los Angeles ham radio operator, was also approached and given the same instructions. To be sure, these requests relative to the disappearance of Amelia Earhart appear quite odd and unnecessary given that the government had already stated she was but a civilian pilot who crashed into the Pacific Ocean.

A formal request was sent to Japanese officials to allow American ships and aircraft to enter the Marshall Island group to search for the Electra, but it was denied. The Japanese informed the Americans that they would conduct their own search with the Twelfth Squadron's four ships, led by the ships *Kamoi* and *Kosyu*.

It was learned later that while the Japanese were informing the world they were actively searching for the downed aviatrix, the Twelfth Squadron, save the *Kosyu*, which was docked at Jaluit, had never left the homeport at Ise Bay, Japan.

The Japanese did not want the U.S. Navy anywhere near the Marshall and Gilbert Islands. They intended for their military installations on these islands to remain secret as long as possible. Japanese foreign minister Koki Hirota ordered Consul General Fukuma to meet with the American naval officer in command of the Earhart search effort. The U.S. officials assured Fukuma that no searches would be conducted near any of the Japanese mandated islands. The Japanese were concerned that the truth had leaked out somehow and were worried that the Americans would press them for details. After the passage of several days, however, no queries arrived.

It was estimated that the cost of the search exceeded $4,500,000. The involvement of the U.S. military in the search for Earhart and Noonan generated severe criticism from some members of Congress. Pennsylvania representative Charles I. Faddis asked the question: "Do you suppose the navy would spend 250,000 dollars a day to hunt for some poor fisherman, perhaps the father of a family, if he were lost in the Pacific?" Representative Byron Scott of California stated, "It is time someone in authority announced that henceforth the navy would not be used to search for 'publicity-stunt' aviators." The notion had been advanced that the United States was anxious to locate and retrieve the Electra before the Japanese found it and discovered the secret cameras.

Two months following the disappearance of Earhart, George Palmer Putnam requested permission from the Japanese to search the Marshall Islands for evidence of her downed plane. He had made a request earlier but was summarily denied. In part, Putnam's letter asked, "Is there any way of ascertaining what the Japanese are actually doing, especially as regards a real search of the eastern fringe of the Marshall Islands? That is one of the most fruitful possible locations for wreckage." The question must be asked: What did Putnam know or suspect that others did not? Or perhaps more accurately, what did Putnam know that the government refused to reveal?

From San Francisco, Consul General Shiozaki cabled Minister Hirota about the request. He stated that Putnam was convinced the Electra could be found at or near the Marshall Islands. Hirota placed Vice Foreign Minister Kensuke Horiuchi in charge of the matter. Horiuchi passed the request on to Admiral Isoroku Yamamoto, the vice minister of the Japanese navy. In a return message to Horiuchi, Yamamoto wrote: "In regard to the search for the remains of the Earhart plane in our mandated territory, our Imperial nation will have all the vessels and fishing boats in the area make every possible effort to search for the remains." The message clearly was intended to stall or deter any effort by Putnam. The Japanese, in truth, had no intention of conducting a search of any kind.

In the end, no evidence was ever produced to suggest the presence of the Electra on land or in water in the area of the search.

Even though the U.S. government officially called an end to the search for Amelia Earhart, evidence exists that indicates that, in one form or another, it continued for years afterward.

· 25 ·

The Mystery of the *Itasca* Logs

$\mathcal{A}$lmost from the time of Earhart's disappearance, the logs of the *Itasca* have been the subject of controversy. Researchers have expressed considerable doubt relative to the accuracy of the records and reports as well as their completeness.

In August 2000, John P. Riley had an article published in *Naval History Magazine* in which he stated that the deck logs of the *Itasca* relative to the Earhart disappearance had been "partially falsified" and that the Howland Island radio log was phony. Riley learned the latter from the Howland Island radio station operators Yau Fai Lum and Ah Kin Leong. Lum told Riley that the entries were "completely fictitious." Lum's name was even misspelled on the logs.

When Riley showed Lum copies of the Howland Island log that indicated he had maintained a radio watch with Radioman Second Class Frank Cipriani, Lum stated that he had never worked with Cipriani and that he had never been assigned any such watch.

The *Itasca*'s chief radioman Leo G. Bellarts related years later that the direction finder used on Howland Island was inoperative and had been disabled when the operator, Frank Cipriani, broke it. The direction finder had been carried aboard the ship, where it was disassembled and inspected by Bellarts. Bellarts found a wire broken by Cipriani and also discovered that the batteries had apparently failed during Earhart's flight as a result of overloading.

Bellarts also reported that documents were mysteriously disappearing from the *Itasca*'s central radio headquarters. He reported the disappearances, and a short time later his commanding officer instructed him to secure the room. Who was taking the documents and why remains a mystery to this day, but it must be assumed with a degree of certainty that such orders came from higher up the chain of command.

Documents and journals maintained by radioman Leo G. Bellarts were handed down to his son, David, who in turn provided them to Earhart researchers. From these materials it has been learned that Earhart never attempted to contact the *Itasca* until the last few minutes of the flight. It would have been a simple matter to do so. The question is why?

Louis Ream was a deputy to General William Donovan, who went on to direct the Office of Strategic Services in World War II. Ream was later connected with Allen Dulles, the director of the Central Intelligence Agency. John Ream, Louis's nephew, stated, "It was well known within high ranking intelligence circles that Miss Earhart, at the time of her disappearance, was involved in an intelligence-gathering operation . . . ordered at the request of the highest echelons of government." Ream went on to state that there were "serious blunders by the Navy in their attempt to provide Miss Earhart with proper guidance, and the Navy was and is determined to conceal their participation in their part of the operation."

· 26 ·

On to Saipan

$\mathcal{O}$ver the decades since Earhart's disappearance, a number of theories have evolved relative to her fate as well as that of Fred Noonan; the predominant ones were reviewed in chapter 22. In his 1960 book, *Daughter of the Sky*, author Paul Briand advances a scenario wherein Earhart and Noonan undertook a forced landing near Saipan in the Mariana Islands. There, according to Briand, they were arrested and executed as spies a short time later. Few Earhart researchers have been attracted to Briand's theory, but those that are don't waver. Briand's hypothesis, however, is based on the testimony of a single Saipan native who reported spotting a white woman wearing men's clothes some time prior to the onset of World War II.

Though the evidence to support Earhart and Noonan crash-landing on Saipan is weak, there is little doubt that the two were on the island, having been delivered to the Japanese headquarters located there following their capture at Mili Atoll.

Shortly after being transported to one of the atolls associated with Truk Lagoon on the Caroline Islands, Earhart and Noonan were transferred to a Japanese navy seaplane and flown to Saipan, located northeast of Guam. Truk Lagoon was 2,800 miles west-northwest of Howland Island and almost due north of Lae, New Guinea, from where they had taken off on July 2. Truk Lagoon was another of the Japanese mandated islands.

Further evidence of the transfer of Earhart and Noonan to Saipan comes from U.S. Navy Commander Paul Bridwell. Bridwell states that documentation exists relative to the "transport of Earhart and Noonan from the vicinity of Majuro, Ailinglapalap, and Jaluit Atolls in the Marshals to Yap and then to Saipan." This documentation was found in the radio logs of the USS *Goldstar*, USS *Blackhawk*, USS *Henderson*, and USS *Chaumont* (later named the *Oglala*). Bridwell reports that these vessels intercepted coded messages sent by Japanese ships and shore installations to the home islands of Japan.

On the day the seaplane arrived at Saipan, eleven-year-old Josephine Blanco was walking to Tanapag Harbor to deliver lunch to her brother-in-law, J. Y. Matsumoto. Tanapag Harbor was bustling with activity overseen by the Japanese military and oriented toward improving the docking facilities for larger ships.

According to Blanco, as she approached the harbor she heard the sound of an airplane and looked up to see a twin-engine craft aiming for a landing in the harbor. Since the Electra had been transported to Saipan aboard the *Kosyu*, Blanco was mistaken in her identity of the aircraft and confusing another craft with Earhart's plane. Several minutes later when she finally located her brother-in-law, he told her to come with him to see the "American woman."

The two soon joined a throng of onlookers where they observed an American woman wearing trousers and a shirt similar to a man's. The man wore a short-sleeved shirt. The two Americans, according to Blanco, appeared quite sick; their faces were drained of color and they looked drawn and stressed. Following a short glimpse of the captives, Blanco and Matsumoto watched as the pair was led away by soldiers. Blanco was convinced they were on their way to be executed. The two were, in fact, eventually transported to the Garapan prison, where they were incarcerated.

Earhart and Noonan were first taken to a three-story building named the Hotel Kobayashi Royokan, which had been commandeered to serve as headquarters for Japanese officers and administration. The hotel was owned by a Japanese family named Kobayashi (also spelled Kobayi in some references) who had settled on the island years earlier. Following a round of questions and paperwork, the two prisoners were separated and transferred to the nearby prison.

Ramon Cabrera, who worked as a guard at the prison, told an interviewer that he remembered Earhart and Noonan well and that he was present when they were first brought to their cells. Both had been blindfolded, and their hands were tied behind their backs. At the time, Cabrera thought Earhart was a young-looking man. Jesus Salas, a prisoner at Garapan, also recalled seeing Earhart and Noonan, but only once.

A witness interviewed by author Fred Goerner—Joaquina Cabrera—stated she had seen "a white lady and a man" being held prisoner in the Kobayashi Royokan Hotel in Garapan. She claimed the man was "taken away" and that the woman "was dead of disease."

In a 1970 interview, Michiko Segura, the daughter of the Garapan chief of police, told the story that Japanese military police shot Amelia Earhart as a spy in 1937. Segura was eleven years old when she heard soldiers describing the execution to her father.

In 1961, José Pangelinan told interviewer Fred Goerner of seeing an American man and woman on Saipan, but never together. The man, he said, was held in the prison, and the woman resided "at the hotel in Garapan." Pangelinan claimed the man was beheaded and the woman died of dysentery. He admitted he was an eyewitness to neither of the two events.

Grigorio Camacho, a brother-in-law of Josephine Blanco, was interviewed years later. At the time of the interview he was a retired judge. He stated that Noonan resisted his captors. He also said that at the time Saipan was occupied by the Japanese, it was expected of the families of prisoners to provide them nourishment. As a result, Earhart and Noonan, he claimed, were fed little but watery soup. Both became ill with dysentery.

Camacho stated that Noonan, angered at his treatment by the Japanese, went into a rage one afternoon and threw his bowl of soup in the face of his guard. Camacho said the navigator was taken some distance from the prison and executed.

Earhart was regularly walked from her cell at the prison to the administration offices in the hotel for questioning. During these transfers, Earhart was often seen by the native Saipanese. Matilda Fausto Arriola, during an interview, recalled that her family gave Earhart fresh fruit because they suspected she was suffering from dysentery. Arriola stated that the "white woman" was a brunette and her hair was cut short like a man's. Arriola also said that the woman gave her sister a "gold ring with a white stone."

Ana Villagomez Benevente worked as a maid at the administration building and was given the job of washing the woman's clothes. Benevente said that she often saw the woman seated on one of the verandas of the upper floors. She said the woman had short, wavy hair.

Benevente also saw the woman "at least three times" at the Garapan prison, where she often went to visit her brother. She was unable to get close to the woman because of the ever-present guards.

Another Saipanese woman, Maria Roberta de la Cruz, said she was informed that the two flyers were Americans and had crash-landed near an island to the south. A Catholic nun who resided on the island recalled that she was told that the woman was caught for spying and that her name was Amelia.

Concepcion Díaz, an early owner of the Kobayashi Royokan Hotel, related that a woman matching Earhart's description had been imprisoned there by the Japanese from some time in 1937 until she died in 1938.

Father Sylvan Conover, a Catholic priest assigned to Saipan, took the story of an elderly female resident of the island who stated she saw "a white woman being transported from Aslito Field in the sidecar of a Japanese motorcycle." An accompanying motorcycle transported in its sidecar a "white man with a large bandage around his head." Both had their hands tied and were clearly prisoners.

In 1937, a seven-year-old Saipanese named Anna Magofo watched two Japanese soldiers guarding a white man "with a big nose" and a white woman while they were digging a hole just outside the cemetery near Garapan City. When interviewed as an adult, Magofo claimed the man was then blindfolded, beheaded, and placed in the hole. Magofo led a group of Earhart researchers to the spot she was convinced was the grave. When it was excavated, found among the debris were a three-tooth gold dental bridge and a number of bone fragments. Later, an anthropologist determined that the bones had belonged to "a female, probably white individual, between . . . forty and forty-two [years of age]." Other bones found belonged to a male. No evidence was ever produced to suggest it was Amelia Earhart and/or Fred Noonan interred in the grave.

By mid-1938, word had spread throughout the city of Garapan that the white woman prisoner had died of dysentery. The rumor was never substantiated, and proof of her demise was never forthcoming.

Two Saipan women—Florence Kirby and Olympio Borja—related a story they heard from a farmer who had an odd experience. As he was retrieving a cow that was tethered at the end of his pasture, the farmer saw several Japanese soldiers marching a man and a woman toward the Garapan cemetery. The prisoners, he said, had their hands tied behind their backs, were wearing khaki uniforms, and had bags tied over their heads. Their exposed skin suggested they were white. On seeing the Japanese, the farmer, fearful of being spotted by the soldiers, ducked out of sight and remained hidden for several hours. He was convinced, he said, that the Japanese executed the two prisoners.

A short time later, a Japanese policeman who was dining with his thirteen-year-old daughter was interrupted by several other Japanese police officers who boasted of killing two Americans—a man and a woman.

Kirby and Borja also related that their grandfather, who was a prisoner at Garapan, occupied a cell near the one "occupied by the American lady pilot." For years, when tourists visited Saipan, they were directed toward the prison where they could see Amelia Earhart's cell.

When American soldiers invaded Saipan in 1944, a number of photographs of Amelia Earhart were found. Ralph R. Kanna, a soldier from Johnson City, New York, found a photograph of Earhart standing beside a Japanese airplane. Kanna gave the photograph to an intelligence officer. Another soldier—Robert Kinley from Norfolk, Virginia—came upon a photograph of Earhart standing next to a Japanese officer. The background in the photograph contained landmarks sufficient to indicate it was taken on the island of Saipan.

Corporal Harry Weiser came across a photograph of Earhart in a Saipan house he inspected. It was subsequently identified as one of a quantity she carried with her for publicity purposes.

In addition to the above, numerous other reports, as well as rumors, exist pertaining to Earhart-related possessions and other evidence. Most, if not all, of these items were turned over to military authorities, where they subsequently disappeared or were classified as top secret by the U.S. government. None of the alleged photographs of Earhart found on the island of Saipan, and there were several, have ever surfaced.

Following the U.S. military occupation of Saipan, a number of rumors arose relative to the notion that the U.S. Marines were led by natives to a place where Earhart and Noonan had been buried. Under orders, the rumors continued, the marines dug up the remains and had them shipped to the United States. The U.S. Marine Corps denied any involvement in such activity. When questioned, Japanese authorities denied that Earhart and Noonan ever fell into their hands.

The question has been raised: Why would the Japanese not simply return Earhart and Noonan to the American authorities? To do so would have generated goodwill. During this time, however, the Japanese activity relative to establishing military bases, airfields, ports, and other activities pertinent to their plans to gain control of the Pacific were done in secrecy. The last thing they wanted the rest of the world to know was what they were up to. If Earhart and Noonan had seen such military installations and reported on them, then Japan's secret military preparations would have been exposed.

· 27 ·

The Mystery Letter

$\mathscr{A}$n odd event occurred almost five months after Amelia Earhart disappeared in the Pacific, one that has never been explained and that perplexes researchers to this day. It represents one more mystery in what would come to be a growing number of unsolved and perplexing enigmas revolving around the Earhart disappearance.

On November 27, 1937, an unclaimed letter in the Jaluit post office in the Marshall Islands came to the attention of a man named Carl Heine. Heine was a German missionary and an occasional special correspondent for a variety of publication outlets. The address on the letter was:

Amelia Earhart (Putnam)
Marshall Islands (Japanese)
Radak Group, Maleolap Island (10)
South Pacific Ocean

In the upper left hand corner where a return address is customarily located was printed:

Hollywood Roosevelt Hotel
Hollywood, California

The postal date stamp contained the information "Los Angeles, California" along with the date October 7, 10:00 p.m. Written across one corner of the envelope were the words "Deliver Promptly." The back of the envelope contained the word "Incognito" that was hand-printed in small letters with a very fine touch, decidedly feminine. The letter was unopened.

This envelope is immediately curious due to the fact that virtually everyone in the world, and in particular in the United States, was aware that Amelia Earhart was listed by the U.S. government as having perished when, as it claimed, her plane went down somewhere near Howland Island. The reported crashing and sinking of the Electra occurred just over three months prior to the date on the envelope.

Questions that must be asked include: How did the sender know that Earhart had, in fact, been transported to Jaluit Island? Maleolap is a neighboring island and may have been where mail was sent. And, importantly, who sent the letter?

What is known is that Earhart's personal secretary, Margo DeCarie, was residing in the Hollywood Roosevelt Hotel during the months of September and October in 1937. Did DeCarie know something of the whereabouts of Earhart that was unknown to the U.S. government and the general public? Or perhaps it was information kept under wraps by the government. And if so, how would DeCarie have obtained knowledge of Earhart's stay, however temporary it might have been, on Jaluit?

The number 10 found on the address is baffling. Some researchers have attempted to link the number with the name of the aircraft piloted by Earhart; the Electra was formally known as the Lockheed 10.

What became of the mysterious letter has never been learned. If it had ever been opened and the contents examined, that information was never made available.

· 28 ·

Death or Transfer?

*O*ver time, an abundance of evidence surfaced that suggested Amelia Earhart and Fred Noonan had been incarcerated on the island of Saipan. A handful of unverified accounts allude to the notion that they may have been executed. On July 2, 1960, the *San Francisco Chronicle* carried an article claiming "the famed aviatrix and her navigator . . . crash-landed in Saipan Bay in July, 1937, and were executed by the Japanese." This information was provided by KCBS radio personality turned Earhart researcher Fred Goerner. While initially generating some interest and attention, public interest soon faded when it became clear that Goerner's hypothesis had little to no credibility. Goerner's "proof" of his statements consisted of "rusty parts of a pre-war plane and recorded conversations with natives." The ultimate truth, however, was that the evidence presented for the existence of the Electra consisted solely of a "coral-coated generator skin divers hauled up from the depths of Saipan Bay."

On July 6, the *Chronicle*, in a front-page article, proclaimed that "Japanese photographs and the affidavits of 72 witnesses prove that Amelia Earhart and her navigator, Fred Noonan, were executed on Japanese-held Saipan island in 1937." Earhart researcher Paul Briand informed interviewers that the graves of Earhart and Noonan had been located. Briand made this statement based entirely on what turned out to be insufficient evidence. In short, it was only his opinion that the graves had been found. From all appearances, Briand's conclusion was more the result of wishful thinking than actual research and investigation.

A short time later, former Japanese Imperial Navy captain Zenshiro Hoshina responded to the article from his home in Tokyo stating that the published articles were in error. He said, "No such execution could have taken place without my knowledge and approval." He added that the governor of Saipan would never have undertaken the executions of Americans without authorization from Tokyo and that it never happened.

As it turned out, the information presented in the July 6 article was deemed false. Air Force officer Joe Gervais conceded that photographs he possessed were "not really proof of Miss Earhart's execution." Further, he also admitted that the "72 affidavits that allegedly proved Earhart and Noonan were executed by the Japanese did not actually describe any executions." They were, Gervais explained, only "72 names of people living today on Saipan and Guam who claimed to have information on the subject."

Then, on July 9, the *Chronicle* reported that the generator Fred Goerner claimed came from Earhart's Electra was bogus. According to an official of the Bendix Aviation Corporation, the company that manufactured the generator for the Electra, the one located by Goerner had been made by a Japanese firm in Osaka. In fact, this was the second generator Goerner claimed belonged to the Electra. It was beginning to appear as though Goerner was fabricating evidence designed to make him appear as a dogged, competent, and successful researcher when, in fact, he was not.

In the final analysis, there exists no credible evidence and no support that Earhart or Noonan crash-landed at Saipan or had been executed on that island. There does, however, exist a body of compelling evidence indicating that they were transported to Saipan from where the Electra came down in the Marshall Islands and that they were held prisoner there for a time. Though stories abound relative to the executions and interment of Earhart and Noonan on Saipan, not a single shred of credible information has ever surfaced to suggest that these executions ever occurred.

The truth is, no one ever saw the corpse of anyone positively identified as either Earhart or Noonan. Sites alleged by some to be the graves of one or both of the Americans have been dug up. In some cases nothing was ever found, and in other cases bones were encountered, but, despite claims to the contrary, none were ever identified as having belonged to Earhart or Noonan.

What, then, became of the prisoners? The most reliable evidence suggests that after a period of incarceration on Saipan, they were transferred to Tokyo and then on to a prison camp in China.

Earhart's presence in Tokyo is controversial and oft debated. In 1972, then secretary of state James Baker confirmed the existence of a State Department file titled "Amelia Earhart: Special War Problems." According to information obtained, the file reveals that Earhart, while a prisoner of Japan, might have participated in that nation's development and construction of aircraft. According to the report, Earhart may have been involved in test-flying aircraft and participating in wind tunnel experiments. The report also describes that Earhart had filed for Japanese "naturalization" in August 1939. When pressed, Secretary Baker refused to explain why such a file existed at all for someone who, according to the government, "disappeared without a trace" in 1937.

Arthur DeWayne Gibson, an archivist for the U.S. State Department, found a letter in departmental files dated August 1939 that stated: "Mrs. Putnam wishes the United States Government to henceforth consider her a National of the Nipponese Imperial Islands."

Gibson also encountered other Earhart-related documents in the secret files. One mentioned that the aviatrix was involved in aircraft design and testing in Tokyo during the year 1939. She was working closely with famous Japanese airplane designer Jiro Horikoshi. During a period of research, it was discovered that Earhart had met Horikoshi years earlier in Long Island, New York, during the time he was visiting the Curtiss-Wright aircraft factory there.

Gibson also found a reference to the notion that by 1939, Earhart could speak fluent Japanese. In addition, the files yielded a photograph of Earhart standing next to a Japanese prototype fighter plane that had been designed and tested around 1939 but never placed into mass production.

On June 11, 1975, Air Force officer and Earhart researcher Joe Gervais sent a letter to the Nipponese Department of Immigration and Naturalization in Tokyo. He requested the date on which "Mrs. G. P. Putnam became a citizen of Japan, probably sometime between July and September of 1939 after she completed the required twenty-four-month residence in the Nipponese Imperial Islands of the Pacific."

On July 7, 1975, Gervais received a response from Japan's Naturalized Citizens Department. The letter acknowledged "receipt of your letter of inquiry. . . asking us whether Irene Craigmile or Mrs. G. P. Putnam was naturalized to Japan." The letter writer went on to say that "we are not in a position to answer any inquiry as to whether a certain person was naturalized to Japan . . . the records of naturalized persons being closed to the public." What is bizarre, and rather telling, about this response is that, in his letter, Gervais never once mentioned the name Irene Craigmile, a name that will factor heavily into the mystery of what happened to Amelia Earhart.

· 29 ·

The Mystery of Wilbur Rothar

$\mathcal{A}$ man named Wilbur Rothar entered the realm of mystery surrounding Amelia Earhart's disappearance during the summer of 1937. Rothar would be easy to dismiss as one of several crackpots who managed to find his way into the Earhart puzzle if it weren't for some odd tangents to his bizarre case.

Shortly after the disappearance of Amelia Earhart, her husband, George Palmer Putnam, offered a $2,000 reward for information leading to the rescue of his wife and Fred Noonan. In August 1937, Wilbur Rothar, using the alias of Johnson, appeared at Putnam's New York office with a strange tale and a request for the money.

According to Rothar, Earhart and Noonan were found on a small island not far from New Guinea by a group of men in a vessel that was illegally transporting arms to Spain. Rothar, a.k.a. Johnson, informed Putnam that he had been employed as a member of the vessel's crew. During the voyage, claimed Rothar, the vessel stopped at a small island to take on fresh water. In a tiny cove, he said, they found the wreckage of the Electra. Earhart was unharmed but Noonan, who had been injured during the crash, had succumbed to a shark attack. Earhart was rescued and taken aboard the vessel, where she was examined by a Chinese doctor. At the time, stated Rothar, no one knew the identity of the woman. Days later after arriving in Panama, the gunrunners recognized her from newspaper articles pertaining to the disappearance. They were afraid to put her ashore because they feared she would be identified and that officials might want to examine the boat that was filled with illegal arms. They sailed instead to New York, where they intended to collect the reward.

As proof, Rothar offered Putnam a scarf that had allegedly been worn by the aviatrix. The skeptical Putnam asked Rothar if he could provide him with a lock of Amelia's hair so that there would be no doubt. Rothar said that he would, and the two men agreed to meet at the same location the following day. It was not learned whether Rothar provided a lock of hair, but Putnam paid him $1,000 in cash with a promise that the balance would be provided when Amelia was released into his custody. Rothar agreed to the proposition. Within an hour, he was arrested for extortion.

The subsequent police investigation of Rothar yielded the information that he was forty-two years old, lived in the Bronx, New York, under the name Goodenough, and was employed as a janitor. Prior to finding this job he was employed as a woodworker. According to the police report, Rothar was married and had eight children.

Rothar was arraigned in felony court on August 5 and scheduled to face a New York County grand jury. The involvement of Wilbur Rothar in the Earhart saga appeared ready to be filed away as nothing more than a deranged and ill-conceived plot that had gone awry, one concocted by a troubled man. But it was only just beginning to take some curious turns and provide yet another layer of mystery to what would become a complex, growing, and puzzling array of mysteries associated with the Earhart disappearance.

According to the article about Rothar's extortion attempt and subsequent arrest, the *New York Times* reported that it learned the suspect came into possession of the scarf three years earlier. Rothar had traveled to Roosevelt Field in Long Island in the hope of seeing Amelia Earhart, who was making a scheduled and well-publicized landing there. Rothar was only one in a large crowd that showed up at the airfield to view the aviatrix and try to obtain her autograph. As Earhart was climbing from her plane, a gust of wind blew the brown and white scarf she was wearing off her shoulders and into the hands of Rothar. The scarf had been in his possession ever since, and it was a scarf identified by Putnam's stenographer as having once belonged to Earhart.

In spite of the account provided by Putnam and in spite of what was reported in the *New York Times* article, Amelia Earhart's sister, Muriel Morrissey, provided a different version. Morrissey claimed Rothar came into possession of the scarf only three months earlier at an airplane hangar at Wheeler Field in Hawaii. How Morrissey would know this, if it is true, is unclear. Morrissey further stated that in spite of the well-publicized $2,000 reward, Rothar demanded $5,000 from Putnam. She also claimed that Putnam, instead of providing Rothar with $1,000 of the reward money with a promise of the balance on the delivery of his wife, merely gave Rothar fifty dollars "for my wife's scarf" and sent him on his way.

It is difficult to account for the differences in the two versions of the same story. One has to wonder how Morrissey came by her information relative to Rothar allegedly picking up Earhart's scarf in Hawaii. One must also wonder why, in Morrissey's account, the established $2,000 reward was changed to $5,000. In her account, Morrissey described Rothar as a "shame-faced and frightened young man." Rothar was forty-two years old, far from being a young man. Morrissey was thirty-seven years old at the time, five years younger than Rothar. And since there is no evidence that Morrissey was present when the events involving Rothar were taking place, how would she know what he looked like at all?

Regarding the scarf, here is another important consideration: until Putnam demanded of Rothar some proof of his Earhart connection, the scarf was never mentioned. Rothar produced it only after Putnam asked for proof. Over the years, the Rothar case was to grow even stranger.

The New York police lost no time in indicting Wilbur Rothar, alias Wilbur Goodenough, alias Wilbur Johnson, for extortion on August 5, 1937. Rothar pleaded not guilty. On August 13, Rothar was transferred to New York's Bellevue Hospital for ten days of "sanity tests." On October 13, a general sessions court committed Rothar to the Matteawan State Hospital for the Criminally Insane to receive treatment prior to being tried on the charge of extortion. Attending the commitment hearing was George Putnam and Special Agent Thomas J. Donegan of the Federal Bureau of Investigation. Rothar's attorney during this time was a man named Edward T. Tighe.

The presence of the FBI was curious, and Donegan's role was never made clear. During the next two decades, Agent Donegan was to assume responsibilities as special assistant to the U.S. attorney general, chairman of internal security on the National Security Council, the FBI representative to the Executive Office of the President of the United States, a member of the Subversive Activities Control Board in Washington, D.C., and administrative assistant to FBI director J. Edgar Hoover. Donegan had also been a lieutenant in the U.S. Naval Reserve. All things considered, Donegan's rapid rise through the higher echelons of governmental administration was truly impressive following his brief involvement in the Rothar-Earhart case. And curious.

In 1966, Donegan was asked a number of questions regarding the case of Wilbur Rothar. For reasons never stated, he refused to answer any of them. In that same year, Rothar's lawyer, Edward T. Tighe, still a practicing lawyer in New York City, similarly refused to respond to Rothar-related queries.

During Rothar's sanity evaluation a strange incident was brought up. According to the evaluator, a Dr. Leonardo, Rothar, in referring to the alleged rescue of Earhart, stated that "the boiler was blown up by ammunition." Leonardo had no idea what Rothar was talking about and assumed he was referring to a boiler on the gunrunning vessel. In truth, "the Boiler" was the nickname for certain Electra models, according to Lockheed Aircraft

Corporation public relations director Philip L. Juergens. The nickname was not known outside of aircraft and pilot personnel, so how would Rothar know this?

According to Earhart researcher and writer Joe Klaas, the law of the state of New York specifies that any prisoner who is under indictment and is committed to a hospital for the criminally insane before his/her trial may neither be transferred nor be dismissed without being returned to the original court to stand trial. Wilbur Rothar was never returned to stand trial for the charge of extortion. Thus, he should have remained incarcerated at the Matteawan State Hospital. If Rothar had not died, he would still have been there in 1965 when researcher Joe Gervais went to look for him. But Rothar was not there.

In response to a letter Gervais wrote to the hospital's superintendent in 1965, he learned that on April 19, 1960, a Wilbur "Rokar" had been transferred to Harlem Valley State Hospital at Wingdale, Duchess County, New York. The superintendent provided no other information on "Rokar."

Rothar had apparently been confined in a New York state mental hospital for over two decades under a similar but different name. Rothar had been transferred illegally, for he had never been brought to trial on the charge of extortion.

Gervais contacted the director of the Harlem Valley State Hospital, a Dr. Lawrence P. Roberts, who informed him that "Rokar" had been transferred to the Central Islip State Hospital on March 23, 1962. Gervais then communicated with CISH director Dr. Francis J. O'Neill, who informed him that "Rokar" had been discharged from the hospital on October 25, 1963. O'Neill said the files contained no information on where "Rokar" might have gone.

New York State law strictly forbids the discharge of a prisoner who is under indictment from a state hospital without having been subjected to a trial. No such trial for Rothar ever took place, adding more strangeness and mystery to this odd event.

Growing ever more curious, Gervais contacted the Suffolk County Police Department inquiring about Rothar, or Rokar. Deputy Commissioner John P. Finnerty replied, stating that their records showed that "Rokar" escaped from the Central Islip State Hospital on October 17, 1962. One year later, "Rokar" returned to the hospital and turned himself in. According to the police records, "Rokar" returned to CISH four days after the hospital records claimed he was discharged. Further investigation into the matter yielded no additional information.

During his investigations, Gervais examined the New York City phone book for any Rothars. Since Rothar left a wife and eight children, the chances were good that one or more of them remained. He could find no listing whatsoever for a Rothar. He also tried Goodenough, the name Rothar was renting his apartment under when he was arrested. None were listed.

Gervais decided to go to Rothar's former apartment to determine whether he could learn anything substantial. The address as provided by Rothar at the time of his arrest was 316 East 155th Street. What Gervais discovered remains perplexing to this day. There is not, and never was, a 316 East 155th Street. Such an address never existed, but this error was apparently never noted by the New York City police and subsequent investigators.

Not to be deterred, Gervais called the Central Islip State Hospital and spoke to a registration clerk inquiring about "Rokar." The clerk advised Gervais that the name was in fact not "Rokar," but "Rakor," and that the records showed he had left the hospital without permission and never returned.

Gervais encountered another odd connection. He learned that after being confined in the Matteawan State Hospital for the Criminally Insane for twenty-three years, Rothar, without ever being returned to trial, was quietly transferred to CISH five days before the publication of the Amelia Earhart–related book *Daughter of the Sky* by Paul Briand. Gervais surmised that the move was made on purpose and in response to the book's release.

Then came another odd event. In response to an inquiry, the administrators of Bellevue Hospital, where Rothar was originally transferred for observation, stated that they had no record of Wilbur Rothar ever having been admitted there in 1937. The hospital did have in its records, however, a notation stating that a Wilbur Rothar was admitted on September 27, 1964, almost a year following his disappearance from CISH, for an "emergency dressing" because of some injury. He was transported to a hospital from the Municipal Lodging House in the Bowery and released the same day.

What became of Wilbur Rothar remains a mystery, one that has never been resolved. Furthermore, what has never been explained was his odd connection to Earhart's disappearance and the subsequent illegal transfers from one hospital to another. Following Rothar's disappearance from the CISH, he was never seen or heard from again, in spite of the fact that the Suffolk County Police Department has in its files a notation that he returned to the CISH on October 29, 1963.

· 30 ·

Tokyo Rose

*W*hile incarcerated on the island of Saipan, Earhart was referred to as "Tokyo Rosa." According to Saipanese Antonio M. Cepeda (also spelled Cepada in some references), who was interviewed by Earhart researcher Joe Gervais, Tokyo Rosa was a term that meant "American spy lady." When showed a photograph of Earhart, Cepeda said it was the same woman who was a prisoner at Garapan. Cepeda's observation was confirmed by another Saipanese, Carlos Palacios, who said "Tokyo Rosa was my people's expression for American spy girl." Like Cepeda, when Palacios was shown a photograph of Earhart, he stated that it was the same woman he saw in captivity on Saipan.

Following the European D-Day, when it was apparent that the Japanese resistance was about to collapse, a woman's voice was often heard broadcasting false information from Tokyo to American GIs. The broadcasts were intended to entice and demoralize the U.S. troops on programs titled "Humanity Calls," "The Postman Calls," "Prisoners Hours," and more. The female voice broadcasting would tell the troops that Japanese fighter planes had wiped out the U.S. Navy and that their wives and girlfriends back in the United States were unfaithful and running around on them. The voice was known throughout the Pacific as "Tokyo Rose."

In her book *Courage Is the Price*, Earhart's sister, Muriel Morrissey, asked, "Could this 'Tokyo Rose' possibly be Amelia, brainwashed to the point of leading her countrymen into enemy traps?" It has been estimated that nine out of ten Pacific-based troops had listened to Tokyo Rose broadcasts.

As a result of suspicion that Tokyo Rose might have been Earhart, George Palmer Putnam, who was fifty-five years old at the time, was provided a direct commission as a major in army intelligence and, with no training whatsoever, was immediately sent to China. Morrissey wrote of Putnam's assignment to China as well as a three-day slog through Japanese-held territory to a Marine Corps radio station where Tokyo Rose broadcasts came in loud and clear. Morrissey stated that Putnam alone "could without question identify Amelia's voice, even though weakened and tense from psychological mistreatment." For the U.S. government to make such an assignment to a civilian suggests they knew something unknown to the rest of the world.

Morrissey's statement "even though weakened" is suspicious. Normally one would say "even if weakened." Did Morrissey know something, as has been suggested? Further, why would the U.S. government provide Putnam the rank of major and ship him across the world to listen to a woman's voice after they spent so much time and energy declaring she crashed and sank in the Pacific Ocean? It was apparent they knew something they were not revealing to the American public.

On July 12, 1949, a woman named Iva Ikuko Toguri D'Aquino was arrested, charged, and tried for treason as Tokyo Rose. During the two months of testimony, it was brought out that there may have been as many as fifteen different women who broadcast as Tokyo Rose. It was also learned that as many as forty female prisoners of war were engaged in preparing and broadcasting the programs. It was rumored that Amelia Earhart was one of the fifteen women who broadcast over the airwaves as Tokyo Rose. According to author David K. Bowman, the U.S. Military Intelligence Service in 1944 was convinced that Earhart was involved in the Tokyo Rose broadcasts.

D'Aquino was an American citizen of Japanese parents, a California resident, and a UCLA coed. She was found guilty and sentenced to ten years at the federal penitentiary in Alderson, West Virginia.

In an interesting aside, it is documented that Amy Otis Earhart, Amelia's mother, attended the Tokyo Rose trial every day. Following the verdict, she told a reporter for the *New York Times* that she knew her daughter "had ended up in Japan's care."

Author Klaas was of the opinion that Amelia Earhart was given the code name "Tokyo Rose" by the Japanese, who planned on using her to blackmail the United States into signing a treaty favorable to Japan. Roosevelt, according to Klaas, rejected the blackmail and refused to demand Earhart's return, for it would be tantamount to admitting to American espionage. Earhart received the treatment afforded to all American spies captured by a foreign power—she was abandoned by her country.

· 31 ·

The Mystery of the Morgenthau Memo

$\mathscr{H}$enry Morgenthau resided in Hyde Park, New York, in the upper part of the state. There he oversaw a one-thousand-acre farm and grew prosperous. One of his neighbors was Franklin D. Roosevelt. The two men soon became acquainted and in time grew to be close friends. Morgenthau's wife likewise was an even closer friend to the president's wife, Eleanor. When Roosevelt was elected governor of New York, he invited Morgenthau to join his administration. Morgenthau soon distinguished himself as an effective and efficient administrator, was unabashedly loyal to Roosevelt, and evolved into the position of close confidant.

Later, when Roosevelt was elected president of the United States, one of the first men he selected to accompany him to the White House was Morgenthau. In the process of organizing his objectives and realigning his priorities, Roosevelt named his good friend secretary of the treasury. As Morgenthau demonstrated competence in his new appointment, Roosevelt granted him greater powers and influence and relied on him for guidance and advice.

According to Earhart researcher Rollin Reineck, Morgenthau "held the financial as well as the operational control over Amelia Earhart's around-the-world adventure." This contention has never been proved, but of Morgenthau's connection to the Earhart mystery there can be no doubt.

Evidence to this effect can be found in a Dictaphone recording between Morgenthau, at the time the secretary of the treasury, and Eleanor Roosevelt's personal secretary, Malvina Scheider. The transcript of the recorded conversation was introduced to the public in 1987; it was included in a book released that year and titled *My Courageous Sister*. The author was Muriel Earhart

Morrissey, Amelia's sister, with assistance from Earhart researcher Carol Osborne. The recording was found in the Franklin D. Roosevelt Presidential Library in Hyde Park, New York.

Because of several revealing comments by Morgenthau on the recording, it remains surprising that this item was never classified, for it clearly shows government involvement in Earhart's around-the-world flight as well as the fact that she was involved in activities above and beyond setting a flight record.

There is a brief but important backstory associated with the Morgenthau memo. On April 26, 1938, Paul Mantz, a former partner of and technical adviser to Amelia Earhart, wrote a letter to Eleanor Roosevelt requesting her influence relative to helping him obtain the official report of the U.S. Coast Guard vessel *Itasca* as it related to Earhart's flight and disappearance. Specifically, Mantz wanted the radio logs of the transmissions between the ship and Earhart during the flight from Lae, New Guinea, to her stated destination of Howland Island.

Mantz never explained to Eleanor Roosevelt, or anyone else, why he wanted the logs. He did explain, however, that when he requested the logs from the Coast Guard he was informed that "the official report could not be released except through certain channels." It was discovered that the Roosevelt administration had prohibited the release of the radio logs and other pertinent information as it pertained to the Earhart disappearance. A further truth is that many of the government materials related to the disappearance of Amelia Earhart are still classified top secret at this writing.

Mantz, well aware that Earhart and Eleanor Roosevelt were good friends, held out the hope that the first lady would be helpful in his quest to obtain the transmissions. Unsure of what to do, Mrs. Roosevelt forwarded Mantz's letter to Henry Morgenthau on May 10. Attached to the missive was a letter from the first lady on White House stationery that stated in part, "Now comes this letter. . . . I don't know whether you can send this man these records, but in any case, I am sending you the letter and let me know whatever your decision may be." The note was signed, "Affectionately, E. R." The tone of Mrs. Roosevelt's note affirmed Mantz's suspicion that an element of secrecy was involved relative to the Earhart disappearance.

On the morning of May 13, Morgenthau called Mrs. Roosevelt on a White House telephone to discuss the Mantz letter. The first lady was not available to take the call, and Morgenthau conversed with her secretary, Malvina Scheider, whose nickname was "Tommy." The entire conversation between Morgenthau and Scheider, taken directly from the transcription, follows:

Hello, Tommy. How are you? This letter that Mrs. Roosevelt wrote me about trying to get the report on Amelia Earhart. Now, I've been given a verbal report. If we're going to release this, it's just going to smear the whole reputation of Amelia Earhart, and my . . . Yes, but I mean if we give it to this one man we've got to make it public; we can't let one man see it. And if we ever release the report of the *Itasca* on Amelia Earhart, any reputation she's got is gone, because—and I'd like to—I'd really like to return this to you.

Now, I know what Navy did, I know what the *Itasca* did, and I know how Amelia Earhart absolutely disregarded all orders, and if we ever release this thing, goodbye Amelia Earhart's reputation. Now, really—because if we give the access to one, we have to give it to all. And my advice is that—and if the President ever heard that somebody questioned that the Navy hadn't made the proper search, after what those boys went through—I think they searched, as I remember it, 50,000 square miles, and every one of those planes was out, and the boys just burnt themselves out physically and every other way searching for her. And if—I mean I think he'd get terribly angry if somebody—because they just went to the limit, and so did the Coast Guard. And we have the report of all those wireless messages and everything else, what that woman—happened to her the last few minutes. I hope I've just got to never make it public, I mean—O.K.—Well, still if she wants it, I'll tell her—I mean what happened. It isn't a very nice story. Well, yes. There isn't anything additional to something like that. You think up a good one. Thank you.

For reasons never explained, Malvina Scheider's responses to Morgenthau's statements were never recorded. A few minutes after speaking with Scheider, Morgenthau placed a call to Assistant Secretary Gibbons of the Treasury Department. The following conversation was found on the same Dictaphone recording:

Morgenthau: I mean we tried—people want us to search again those islands, after what we have gone through. You know the story, don't you?

Gibbons: We have evidence that the thing is all over, sure. Terrible. It would be awful to make it public.

An undated, unaddressed, and unsigned note on White House stationery was also discovered in the same Hyde Park library archives. The note, which was apparently written by Morgenthau's secretary after he had received Mantz's letter, was directed to Eleanor Roosevelt. It read:

Mr. Morgenthau says that he can't give out any more information than was given to the papers at the time of the search of Amelia Earhart. It seems they have confidential information which would absolutely ruin the reputation of Amelia Earhart and which he will tell you personally at a time when you wish to hear it.

He suggests writing this man and telling him that the President is satisfied from his information, and you are too, that everything possible was done.

On May 14, Eleanor Roosevelt wrote a letter to Paul Mantz that stated:

I have made inquiries about the search which was made for Amelia Earhart and both the President and I are satisfied that the information which we have received that everything possible was done. We are sure that a very thorough search was made.

An examination and analysis of the Morgenthau memo is warranted, perhaps necessary.

Near the beginning of the memo, where Morgenthau says he had been given a verbal report, he is likely referring to one that came from *Itasca* commander Warner K. Thompson. It is a matter of record that during the last week of July 1937, Morgenthau flew from Washington, D.C. to Hawaii. The secretary claimed the trip was a vacation, but it is known that once there, he met privately with Thompson. Clearly, the meeting involved a topic that could not be discussed over the telephone or via telegram or letter. The timing of the visit gives one reason to suspect that it had something to do with the Earhart disappearance. One can only guess at what was so important as to demand an in-person visit with a high-ranking government official and the Coast Guard commander.

Early in the conversation with Scheider, Morgenthau says, "Now I've been given a verbal report. If we're gong to release this, it's just going to smear the whole reputation of Amelia Earhart." Clearly, Morgenthau is privy to information related to the Earhart disappearance not made available to the rest of the world, information of such a grave nature that it would damage the reputation of the aviatrix. This validates the notion that Morgenthau, close confidant of President Roosevelt, had knowledge of what happened to Earhart.

Decidedly puzzling, however, is the reference to something that would damage her reputation. What could that possibly have been? What had happened over the course of the nine months since her disappearance that would have to do with damaging her reputation? Or as has been suggested, did the government have proof of Earhart's involvement in the Tokyo Rose broadcasts? Was the government concerned that if the public learned that Earhart was on a mission to photograph Japanese mandated islands they would think less of her? It must be remembered, during those times the word "spy" had a negative connotation among Americans. On the other hand, had Earhart returned safely to the United States with important reconnaissance information, would she not be regarded as a heroine? It seems likely.

No, something else happened, something the government had knowledge of that they were concerned about, concerned that it would ruin Earhart's reputation. It remains a mystery.

Then Morgenthau makes a reference to the notion that "if we ever release the report of the *Itasca* on Amelia Earhart, any reputation she's got is gone."

Despite all of the concern expressed in the foregoing communications, the logs of the *Itasca* were finally made available. On July 5, approximately two and a half months after receiving Paul Mantz's missive, Eleanor Roosevelt received a letter from Morgenthau stating, "We have found it possible to send to Mr. A. Paul Mantz a copy of the log of the *Itasca*, which I think will supply him with all the data he asked for in his letter of June First." The logs of the *Itasca* were mailed to Mantz on July 21 by Rear Admiral R. R. Wesche of the U.S. Coast Guard.

This series of events raises two important questions: First, if, as Morgenthau expressed in his May 13, 1938, telephone call to Malvina Scheider, "any reputation she's got is gone" should the report of the *Itasca* on Amelia Earhart ever be released, then why would it appear to be acceptable to release the logs two and a half months later? A thorough reading of the *Itasca* logs reveals nothing that could damage the reputation of the aviatrix.

The second question that must then be asked is: Were the logs that were released to Mantz the original logs of the Coast Guard vessel, or had they been tampered with? Had passages been deleted? Evidence has surfaced to support the latter contention (chapter 25, "The Mystery of the *Itasca* Logs").

There is a time period between 8:03 a.m. and 8:43 a.m. (Howland Island time) in the *Itasca* logs that shows no transmissions or receptions. This is just before communications ceased altogether, leading the Coast Guard to announce that the Electra had crashed into the Pacific Ocean. Some researchers who have examined the logs are of the opinion that entries during the aforementioned time period were deleted. Some have also suggested that it might have been these same deleted communications that Morgenthau and Thompson discussed in Hawaii during the last week of July 1937. One must wonder whether Morgenthau's comment "what that woman—happened to her the last few minutes" had anything to do with the missing portion of the log. Or did Morgenthau have a hand in determining which portions of the log needed to be deleted?

Regarding the lack of log entries between 8:03 a.m. and 8:43 a.m., it must be remembered that the government explanation was related to the notion that Earhart was lost and was low on fuel. It does not make sense that a pilot in that kind of situation would cease communications with a source that had the potential to direct her to a safe landing area.

Another statement by Morgenthau invites attention. He said, "I know how Amelia Earhart absolutely disregarded all orders, and if we ever release this thing, goodbye Amelia Earhart's reputation." Whose orders did Earhart disregard? Here is a government official, the secretary of the treasury, referring to Earhart's disregard of orders. There can be no question that Earhart was under orders from the United States government. What could she have been ordered to do? There exists abundant evidence to suggest that Earhart was intended to fly over selected Japanese mandated islands and photograph suspected military installations and buildup. Was this something she agreed to do voluntarily, or was she "ordered" to do so? Would a private citizen be subjected to military or government orders? On the other hand, if the federal government had, in fact, subsidized and facilitated Earhart's around-the-world flight as has been suggested, could she have been placed in a position of agreeing to cooperate with the military on a spy mission? It appears to be the only conceivable conclusion.

Then there is Morgenthau's cryptic comment: "what that woman—happened to her the last few minutes, I hope—I've just got to never make it public." Twelve words later, Morgenthau stated, "It isn't a very nice story."

What does "the last few minutes" mean? Is it a reference to the last few minutes the Electra was in the air before coming down or being forced down? Could it be a reference to the last few minutes of Earhart's life? The last few minutes before she and Noonan were captured by the Japanese? What? Why would Morgenthau hope he would never have to make it public, why isn't it "a very nice story?" What horrible thing could have occurred to have generated comments such as these?

If the truth had come out relative to Earhart's reconnaissance mission, that it was backed by the U.S. government with the blessings of President Roosevelt and Secretary of the Treasury Morgenthau, it would have proved embarrassing. It would have had the appearance of the president subjecting a civilian to a dangerous, some would have said reckless, mission wherein her personal safety was at high risk. This could have had a serious impact on Roosevelt's reputation and could have endangered his chances to be elected for a second term. Politicians are far more concerned with their legacy than they are with the truth; it was as true then as it is now.

In spite of ongoing rumors that Earhart was alive and a prisoner of the Japanese, George P. Putnam had her declared dead on January 9, 1939, eighteen months after her disappearance. This is dramatically in contrast to tradition and law, which mandates the passage of seven years before such a determination is made in the absence of a body. Fred Noonan's wife of only a few weeks also had him declared dead.

In a letter dated March 15, 1991, Hawaii senator Daniel Akaka requested pertinent Earhart materials from Secretary of the Treasury Nicholas F. Brady. In part, Akaka's letter states:

> I would like to request that your department retrieve from your files, wherever they may be, all classified information concerning Miss Earhart's last flight. When this information has been assembled, please contact my office so that I may make arrangements for its review.

Akaka even listed the precise reference numbers of said materials and where they could be located in the Treasury Department's storage facility. Secretary Brady held the letter for ten days before finally acting on it. He then sent Akaka a memo stating that the "Morgenthau files have been sent to the National Archives." It is interesting, and perhaps telling, that the Earhart materials were referred to as the "Morgenthau files." Since then, though often searched for, the so-called Morgenthau files have never been located. This represents one more example of the government's refusal to cooperate with anyone interested in researching what happened to Amelia Earhart. It is also another mysterious disappearance of materials related to the Earhart case.

If there were no government involvement, and if there were no deception, and if there were no reason to suspect that clandestine, and perhaps illegal, activities were involved, then why would the federal government classify all of the related documents as top secret and refuse to allow honest and curious Earhart researchers to examine them, to search for and make determinations relative to the truth?

The July 25, 1949, issue of the *New York Times* carried a statement by Mrs. Amy Otis Earhart, Amelia's mother. In the article she said, "Amelia told me many things. . . . But there were some things she couldn't tell me. I am convinced she was on some sort of government mission, probably on verbal orders."

Captain Paul L. Briand, in his book *Daughter of the Sky*, wrote that Earhart and Noonan "had flown over islands in the Japanese mandate which were being illegally fortified, the plane had been shot down by anti-aircraft guns, the pilot and navigator had been taken and held as spies."

Dr. M. L. Brittain, the president of Georgia Tech, had been a passenger aboard the USS *Colorado* during the search for Earhart and Noonan. Brittain stated, "We got the definite feeling that Miss Earhart had some sort of understanding with government officials that the last part of her voyage around the world would be over some Japanese islands, probably the Marshalls." In 1944, Brittain maintained that Earhart had been a prisoner of the Japanese and that she would eventually be liberated and returned to the United States.

· 32 ·

The Mystery at Aslito Airfield

$\mathcal{I}$n 1944, Sergeant Thomas E. Devine was the top noncommissioned officer to First Lieutenant Fritz W. Liebig, commanding officer of the 244th Army Postal Unit, which arrived at Saipan following the defeat of the Japanese there on July 12. The unit was bivouacked at Cape Obiam (also spelled Obyam) at the southern end of the island.

Shortly after arriving at Saipan and getting settled, Liebig requisitioned a jeep and summoned Devine to drive him to Aslito Airfield, a recently captured airfield one-half mile away to the northeast. As they neared the installation, a military policeman halted the jeep and informed Liebig they were not allowed to approach. Liebig responded that he had orders to report there. After examining their identification documents and writing down their names and serial numbers, the MP allowed them to proceed.

On arriving at a cluster of buildings and a hangar at Aslito Airfield (today it is named Isley Airfield), Devine pulled the jeep to a stop near a hangar and out of the way of any potential traffic. At the front of the hangar was stationed a group of enlisted marines positioned as if on guard duty. A man who seemed to be in charge, but neither wearing a uniform nor carrying the required sidearm and dressed in only a white shirt and khakis, appeared to be issuing instructions. As Liebig and Devine climbed out of the jeep, the man approached them and, without identifying himself, informed them that the hangar was off-limits and told Liebig to report to the nearby administration building. Devine waited outside.

As Devine lingered in the shade of the building, a marine officer approached the man in the white shirt and angrily demanded to know why the hangar was off-limits. He then said, "We know Earhart's plane is in there!

120

Our men laid down their lives on the line and now they won't even get credit for finding the plane!" The officer, now accompanied by a handful of others who had just walked up, stated that marine major Wallace Greene had determined that it was Earhart's Electra in the hangar. He was informed that Greene had that very day been promoted to colonel.

The man in the white shirt approached the group and asked the vocal officer for his identification. After writing it down, he turned and walked away. Devine noted that the man had "flattened, pugilistic features, yet was handsome." The marines decided to go to the administration building to deal with the matter. When they left, Devine walked back over to the jeep to await the return of Liebig.

Devine had not been in his position long before a marine guard walked up and told him he would have to move the jeep. Devine asked the guard whether it was true that Earhart's plane was inside the hangar. The guard admitted that it was. By this time, Liebig had finished his business, and the two men returned to Camp Obiam.

During the return trip, Liebig and Devine discussed what had transpired outside of the hangar and wondered how Earhart's plane could be in Saipan when the U.S. Navy had informed the world that it had crashed and sunk near Howland Island two thousand miles to the southeast seven years earlier.

Later that afternoon, Devine encountered two other members of his unit—Sergeant Henry Fritzler and a man whose name he could not remember. Following a brief conversation, the unnamed marine said offhandedly, "They're bringing up Earhart's plane." Devine asked him what that meant, but the marine, believing he was revealing too much information, changed the subject.

A short time later, Devine heard the sound of an airplane approaching the camp. Looking up, he spotted a "twin-engine, double-fin civilian plane." From his position on the ground, Devine could read the identification number. It was NR16020. Clearly, the Electra either survived the crash landing at Mili Atoll or was repaired by the Japanese after it was recovered and transported to Saipan.

Though the members of the unit were not allowed to leave the camp after sundown, Devine decided to take a chance on a clandestine return visit to Aslito Airfield. He invited a friend, Private Paul Anderson, to accompany him. The two men arrived at a point near the southwest corner of the airfield that contained an extended arm of the airstrip. In his book, *Eyewitness: The Amelia Earhart Incident*, Devine wrote:

At the southwest end of the airfield, before a roofless hangar, we saw the twin-engine, double-fin plane which earlier had flown above Camp Obiam. It displayed no military insignia. As we drew closer, a photographer stood up from a crouch. He was facing the plane, apparently photographing it, but was too far away to determine if he were military or civilian. I wanted to speak to him, but as I approached, he ran away.

Near the twin-engine plane, Devine and Anderson spotted several containers of fuel. Moving closer, Devine once again saw the same identification number he had earlier seen on the plane flying over the camp. The two men decided to see whether they could enter the aluminum airplane. Nearing one of the propellers, Devine noted that it bore the inscription "Hamilton Standard."

While trying to determine the best way to get into the Electra, Devine spotted the same photographer again. When the photographer realized he had been seen, he turned and ran away a second time. A moment later, two men emerged from a hangar a short distance away. One was wearing a flyer's helmet and jumpsuit. The other was the man in the white shirt Devine had seen that morning. He was now carrying a bandolier of ammunition across his shoulders. The two men were walking toward two fighter planes that were idling on a nearby landing strip. Devine and Anderson decided it was time to hasten back to their camp.

After showering and preparing to retire for the night in his tent, Devine heard a "muffled explosion" coming from the direction of Aslito Airfield. A second later he spotted a large fire. Curious, he decided to sneak back to the location to have a look.

According to Devine:

The fire roared as I crouched and crawled toward the airfield. When I could see what was burning, I was aghast! The twin-engine plane was engulfed in flames. I could not see anyone by the light of the fire, but I lay very still and watched the blaze. I dared not move lest the fire disclose my presence to an alert sniper.

Suddenly, I was enveloped by a tremendous noise. A plane had taken off and was directly over me. After a slight interval, a second plane followed. Both of them were evidently headed for one of the aircraft carriers off Saipan.

As Devine watched, the two fighter planes sent a fusillade of bullets into the Electra, igniting the fuel and creating an explosion similar to the one Devine heard back at camp. The explosion and fire completely obliterated the identity of the Electra.

Devine concluded that the fuel canisters he had seen earlier were added to the tanks, nearly filling them. More fuel was likely poured into and onto the Electra. In August 2003, sixteen years after the publication of his book that contained an account of the discovery of the Electra, Devine received a letter from a man named Art Beech. Beech told Devine about his uncle as a member of a task force sent to Saipan to "recover what they could of Amelia Earhart, bring her back if she was alive, and destroy everything if she was dead." The uncle recovered "her diary and some other papers."

While on Saipan, according to the letter writer, the uncle saw the Electra in flight on at least two occasions. One day, the uncle was ordered to dump two five-gallon cans of aviation fuel onto and into the aircraft and set it afire. The following day, he watched as a bulldozer pushed what remained of Earhart's Electra into a dump "containing damaged Japanese planes."

Devine pondered the events he witnessed at the Aslito Airfield and wondered at their meaning. Obtaining access to a military publication several weeks later, Devine encountered a photograph of the man in the white shirt. It was Secretary of the Navy James V. Forrestal.

When Forrestal learned of Earhart's Electra being found in the hangar at Aslito Field, he knew he would have to become involved. A brilliant man and a competent administrator, Forrestal knew immediately that this discovery bode ill for future peace efforts and postwar international relations with Japan, not to mention the damage it could cause to the reputations of President Roosevelt, Morgenthau, and others. Any news of the Electra needed to be suppressed.

Forrestal controlled most of the publicity emanating from the U.S. Navy. Prior to the Aslito Airfield incident, Forrestal had made five well-publicized inspection trips to the Pacific, publicity he generated himself. It should be pointed out that when Forrestal made these trips, he normally dressed in khakis and an unbuttoned white shirt. Significantly, while Forrestal kept a concise and up-to-date diary, he entered nothing during the time he was alleged to be in Saipan. The 1944 trip to Saipan generated no publicity, for it would not have been in the best interests of the U.S. government to do so should the report of the existence of the Electra prove to be true. Such news would have resulted in considerable ill will toward the Japanese.

On returning stateside, Devine submerged himself deep into research regarding Amelia Earhart, her disappearance, and the possibility that the government erred in declaring she "crashed and sank" in 1937. Devine wrote a report of his experience at Aslito Airfield in Saipan and submitted it to the Office of Navy Intelligence. He was in possession of some photographs pertinent to his research that he wanted to submit but was informed by the head of the ONI that he was to send them to the security risk agency at the Hartford, Connecticut, Naval and Marine Corps Reserve Training Center.

The obvious question is why, after twenty-three years, would information and/or photographs related to the disappearance of Amelia Earhart be regarded as a security risk?

· 33 ·

The Mystery of James V. Forrestal

James V. Forrestal died on the morning of May 22, 1949, at Bethesda Naval Hospital in Maryland. His death has been referred to as "shocking" and "disturbing." U.S. Navy officials immediately released the information that Forrestal's death was a suicide. According to the report, Forrestal walked into a sixteenth-floor pantry, tied one end of the sash from his bathrobe to a radiator and the other end around his neck, and leaped out the window. Skeptics insist he was murdered and that his death was tied to the disappearance of Amelia Earhart.

Before he had completed two years as Secretary of Defense, James Forrestal was forced to resign by President Harry S. Truman. A short time later, he was taken to the Bethesda Naval Hospital to undergo treatment for "operational fatigue." Following his admission to the facility, he was diagnosed with low blood pressure, anemia, and exhaustion, along with psychiatric symptoms . . . associated with excessive fatigue," by military physicians.

Forrestal was placed in a room on the sixteenth floor of the hospital and virtually held prisoner there. He was allowed visits from no one save his wife and two sons, and even these were difficult to arrange. His attending physician, Captain George M. Raines, refused requests from Forrestal to see anyone else, specifically forbidding access to his brother, Henry, his priest, Father Paul McNally, and Monsignor Maurice S. Sheehy. Sheehy, a close friend, was a former Navy chaplain. Sheehy made at least seven trips to the hospital to see Forrestal but was denied each time. No reason was ever provided. A restricted visitation policy such as this seems extreme for someone diagnosed with symptoms of fatigue. Could it be that a decision had been made to isolate Forrestal as much as possible? And could that decision have had anything to do with the disappearance of Amelia Earhart?

After threatening to go to the press regarding the bizarre regulations pertinent to visiting his brother, Henry was finally admitted. He later stated that Forrestal was in good health, "acting and talking as sanely and intelligently as any man I've ever known." Dr. Raines eventually admitted to the family that Forrestal was "fundamentally all right." As a result, Henry began making arrangements to check his brother out of the hospital. Only a few hours after initiating the paperwork for Forrestal's release, the former secretary of defense was found dead.

Only moments before Forrestal died, he received a visit from Admiral Husband E. Kimmel. Later, Kimmel was court-martialed and found by a military court to be one of the officers responsible for the lack of preparation relating to the attack on Pearl Harbor. According to records, Forrestal was one of the officers who blamed Kimmel for irresponsibility and lack of preparation related to the disaster. According to the priest who was in attendance on the floor of the hospital, Kimmel ordered the navy corpsman responsible for monitoring Forrestal to leave the room. Kimmel was the last person to see Forrestal alive.

The family of James Forrestal claimed he was not a man capable of committing suicide, that they had made plans to travel to some location in the country to spend time relaxing. Forrestal was looking forward to it and making plans for the trip.

It was later learned that Forrestal, after being removed from his post as secretary of defense, was delivered to Bethesda Naval Hospital under White House orders. There, he was kept in what amounted to solitary confinement, barred from most outside contacts, handled as a patient with an advanced mental condition, and provided "unusual" medical treatment and limited freedom.

In June 1949, Forrestal's widow sought payment of a $10,000 insurance policy, claiming accidental death. Her attorneys argued for payment, maintaining in spite of the official report that the navy secretary's death did not involve suicide. The details of Forrestal's death in 1949 were suppressed by the U.S. government. From 1949 until 2004, they were classified as top secret. Again, these are extreme measures related to someone allegedly suffering from fatigue and related symptoms.

In 2004, after invoking the Freedom of Information Act, a newsman named David Martin was provided access to "the full report of the investigative review board appointed the day after Forrestal's death." It was named the Willcutts Report. The report contained the odd conclusion that the U.S. Navy was in no way responsible for Forrestal's death, a statement that seemed somewhat defensive and unnecessary. A second odd aspect of the report is that, though the government claimed Forrestal committed suicide, the report did not cite suicide as the cause of death. The fact that the government refused to release the contents of the report for forty-five years invites suspicion.

Martin, an investigative reporter and news analyst, conducted his own inquiry into Forrestal's death. He discovered that the results and witness testimony compiled and reported by the U.S. Navy was kept secret and that the entire event was "replete with deceptions." From his own investigation, which included interviewing many of the same witnesses as did the government, Martin concluded that Forrestal had been murdered and that government collusion was involved.

An examination of the method by which Forrestal allegedly committed suicide is warranted. The U.S. government press release stated he had tied one end of his bathrobe sash to a radiator, tied the other end around his neck, and leaped out a sixteenth-floor window. This could not have been possible. Providing a generous length of six feet for a bathrobe sash, an experiment conducted on November 6, 2013, revealed that the knots necessary for attachment to a radiator and a human neck would take up approximately four feet of the sash, leaving only two feet. Assuming the radiator was located conveniently beneath the window Forrestal allegedly jumped out of, the two feet of remaining sash would not allow the former Naval officer enough length to stand upright, much less leap out of a window. This entire explanation offered by the government was a lie.

Interestingly, there exist other versions of Forrestal's death. Earhart researcher and author Thomas E. Devine states that Forrestal "fell" from the sixteenth floor of the naval hospital. Yet another account refers to Forrestal as leaping "from the sixteenth floor window to the third floor bridge that connected the two wings of the hospital." What this indicates is that there remains a significant amount of confusion related to the mysterious death of James V. Forrestal.

With Forrestal's death went his version of what might possibly have occurred on the island of Saipan in relation to Amelia Earhart's airplane.

· 34 ·

The Electra Mystery

$\mathcal{T}$o this day, controversy surrounds the actual airplane manned by Earhart and Noonan on the around-the-world flight. The XC-35 Electra was constructed by Lockheed and test-flown on May 7, 1937, just prior to Earhart's famous flight. In that year, the XC-35 won Lockheed the Collier Trophy, given for the most valuable contribution to aircraft. The XC-35 represented a significant advancement in flight at the time, but following the disappearance of Earhart on July 2, 1937, production was discontinued. According to author and researcher Joe Klaas, "No record exists today as to what final disposition was made of the XC-35."

Prior to the commencement of Earhart's around-the-world flight, she was photographed on several occasions in the cockpit of the XC-35. Close examination of the photographs, however, reveals that they were cockpits of two different airplanes. The instrument panels were markedly different. Among Earhart researchers, there are some who contend that such modifications were made relative to the alleged spy mission.

The notion of there being two XC-35s used by Earhart has also been advanced on the basis of other photographic evidence. In some photographs, Earhart's aircraft is equipped with fixed-pitch propellers without spinners. In other photographs, "the propellers are hubbed with spinners such as are used to streamline the feathering gear of variable-pitch props." This has led some researchers to suggest that not one, but two Lockheed XC-35s were associated with Earhart's flight.

Author Klaas has suggested that one of the XC-35s was the one in which Earhart and Noonan were flying, the one that was allegedly in the vicinity of Howland Island on July 2, 1937. The other, he suggested, was flown by an American man and woman and was reported to have crashed in the bay at Saipan.

Author Klaas argues that Earhart could not have flown from Lae, New Guinea, to Howland Island in the airplane in which she took off in Miami. It would not fly that fast or that far, insists Klaas. Somewhere between Miami and New Guinea, he says, the XC-35s were switched. With assistance from fellow researcher Joe Gervais, Klaas identified a number of differences between the two planes.

1. Some photographs of the Electra show the CAA registration number as NR16020. In other photos, it is R16020.
2. Photographs show different positions for the port and starboard wingtip navigation lights. In some photos, the lights "were located halfway between the leading and trailing edges and well in front of the curved wingtip." In other photographs, the lights were mounted "jutting out from the forward part of the wingtip."
3. In some photos, the Electra manifests painted engine cowlings, but in others, no paint is visible.

Author Thomas Devine has also acknowledged a number of differences in the early-flight Electra and the one photographed during latter stages of the flight. However, he insists that none of the differences (modification for greater fuel capacity, etc.) proves that the aircraft was equipped for a spy mission. In explaining the differences in the serial numbers, Devine explained that the *N* was not painted on airplanes unless national boundaries were to be crossed.

Based on available newsreel footage of various landings and takeoffs of the Earhart-Noonan flight around the world, including the final liftoff from Lae, New Guinea, it appears that the same plane was employed each time by the aviatrix. However, there may have been a second Electra in the air at the time in the Pacific. According to author James Donahue, there exists a likelihood of another Electra, one "sponsored" by the British and piloted by a man and a woman, flying in the region of Japan's mandated islands at the same time.

There is more to add to the mystery of two Electras involved in the Earhart flight. A man named Lloyd Royer, who was employed by Lockheed Aircraft and was involved in preparing Earhart's plane for the around-the-world flight, stated that there were, in truth, two planes that were being worked on at the facility following the aviatrix's ground-loop incident in Hawaii. Both planes, said, Royer, were to be used during the attempt.

· 35 ·

Imprisonment

$\mathcal{T}$oday in the coastal Chinese city of Weifang, Shandong Province, can be found a number of dark, gray, European-style buildings from the nineteenth century. The buildings have been neglected over the past decades and they now manifest peeling walls, broken windows, and sunken foundations. History records this site as the Weihsien Concentration Camp.

When Japan attacked Pearl Harbor in December 1941, it had an immediate effect on Japanese-occupied coastal China. All Westerners living in China and Japan were classified as enemy aliens, rounded up, and interned in prison camps. One of the largest was the Weihsien facility in Weifang.

What information remains available on Weihsien Prison reveals that at its height it housed 2,008 people from more than thirty countries. Three hundred and twenty-seven of them were children. The prisoners were fed rotten meat, thin soup, and two slices of bread per day. Prisoners were tortured for minor infractions, and executions were common.

It was to Weihsien Concentration Camp that many are convinced the prisoner Amelia Earhart was brought and where she remained until the camp was liberated by American military forces on August 17, 1945. According to author Fred Goerner, Admiral Chester Nimitz, one of the leading military figures of the day, was quoted as stating that it was long "known and documented in Washington" that Earhart lived "under the control of Japan long after she was reported missing in 1937." During a tape-recorded conversation with Goerner, Nimitz stated, "I don't understand why [the U.S. government] still won't let people know what happened." U.S. Naval Commander John Pillsbury sent word to Goerner that he "should continue your investigation, and I want to add that, don't you ever give up. You're onto something that will stagger the imagination."

130

According to a few researchers, Amelia Earhart, following her internment in Saipan, was transferred to military headquarters in Tokyo, Japan. There, she may or may not have been forced into broadcasting as Tokyo Rose.

The files of the Federal Bureau of Investigation contain a memo from director J. Edgar Hoover to Carter W. Clarke, Assistant Chief of Staff of the Office of Naval Intelligence. In the memo, dated January 18, 1945, Hoover relates information about Earhart by an unnamed "member of the armed forces" during the latter part of 1944. According to the FBI director, the soldier was in the Philippine Islands prior to the attack on Pearl Harbor. During that time, he and a fellow soldier were being "entertained by some Japanese in a hotel," the walls of which were thin enough to overhear conversation in an adjoining room. As the soldier listened to two Japanese soldiers speaking English, he overheard that "Amelia Earhart was still alive and being detained at a hotel in Tokyo, Japan."

Weeks later, the soldier was taken prisoner by the Japanese and sent to a concentration camp at Bataan, a Philippine province. From his prison guards, this soldier learned that Earhart was still alive and in Tokyo. They also stated, according to the soldier, that they had heard her broadcast as Tokyo Rose over Japanese radio.

At some point, Earhart was transferred to the Weihsien Prison in Weifang, China, where she may have been a resident for as long as six years. On August 17, 1945, the United States military "Operation Duck" involved an Office of Strategic Services team parachuting into the Weihsien Civilian Internment Camp in northeastern China. The OSS was a U.S. wartime intelligence agency. The objective was to liberate the camp, the first of many efforts involving many such camps throughout Japanese-occupied coastal China.

Among the OSS troops was Lt. Jim Hannon. On assisting in the removal of the prisoners from the Weihsien camp, Hannon encountered a woman he referred to as a "lady Yank." The woman had been housed with the Japanese prisoners and was in poor shape, almost comatose. Many are convinced this woman was Amelia Earhart. The aviatrix would have been forty-eight years old.

Within a few days of the liberation of Weihsien Prison, a radiogram was sent from Chungking to George Palmer Putnam via the U.S. State Department to Putnam's address in North Hollywood, California, where he resided between 1935 and 1945. The text of the message was: "Camp liberated; all well. Volumes to tell. Love to mother." The message was unsigned. The message was found in the National Archives in 1975. At the time it was sent, it was never made public, and Putnam never mentioned it to Earhart's mother or to her sister, Muriel.

Those who ascribe to the Earhart-was-not-at-Weihsien-Prison faction of related research have attempted to "prove" that the message was not sent by Earhart but by a would-be writer named Ahmad Kamal. In fact, Kamal, who was listed as a prisoner at Weihsien, did send a message, but it was to Maxwell Perkins, his presumed editor at Charles Scribner's Sons publishing house. There would have been no need for Kamal to communicate with Putnam. At least one book on Earhart has reported the contention that Kamal sent the message to Putnam, but the evidence presented is spurious.

According to Hannon, the "lady Yank" was flown from Weihsien via Tsingtao to a camp in Korea where other American prisoners were transported for assessment and preparation for return to the United States.

· 36 ·

Repatriation

$\mathcal{M}$onsignor James Francis Kelley was a well-known Catholic figure in the United States during the 1940s. He was a university graduate, a psychologist, and a one-time president of Seton Hall University and was well connected with church hierarchy as well as established political figures in the United States and abroad.

Kelley was ordained on July 8, 1928, in Belgium. There he met Archbishop Eugenio Pacelli. Kelley's duties included teaching the English language to Pacelli, who went on to become Pope Pius XII. In 1934, Kelley earned a degree in philosophy at Louvain, Belgium, and later did graduate work in psychology. In 1935 he received his PhD in philosophy and psychology. A short time after that he was appointed head of the Department of Philosophy at Seton Hall College and professor of psychology at Immaculate Conception Seminary in Darlington, New Jersey. In July 1936 he was named president of Seton Hall College. On April 21, 1941, Kelley was named Right Reverend Monsignor by Pope Pius XII.

Not only was Kelley well connected within the realm of the Catholic Church, he also boasted strong political ties. On July 11, 1941, Kelley received a citation and a medal from Secretary of the Treasury Henry Morgenthau for "three years of patriotic service with integrity and diligence for the Treasury Department of the USA." No details relative to why this award was presented have ever been located.

In December 1941, Kelley met with Secretary of the Navy Frank Knox. A short time later, Kelley, with the assistance of Archbishop Francis Spellman, was appointed chaplain for the Atlantic Overseas Air Command. Spellman maintained close connections with every U.S. president from Franklin D. Roosevelt to Harry S. Truman as well as a number of cabinet members, other political appointees, and military leaders. To many of them he introduced Kelley.

Kelley's acquaintances and friends also included President Franklin D. Roosevelt, General Jonathan Wainwright, J. Edgar Hoover, President Harry S. Truman, Margaret Truman, Charles Lindbergh, and a number of sports celebrities and movie actors.

Based on the available evidence, it appears that Monsignor Kelley entered the Earhart controversy at the invitation of Spellman, who had been advanced to the position of cardinal in the church. On August 14, 1945, Spellman flew from New York City to Honolulu, where he met with Admiral Nimitz. The following day, he met with long-time Earhart friend Jackie Cochran. The reason for Spellman's long trip and his presence at this meeting, along with Cochran's, has never been revealed, but the timing in relation to the pending liberation of the Japanese prison camp in Weifang seems beyond coincidence.

On August 17, the "unidentified" woman believed to be Amelia Earhart was encountered and rescued from a Japanese prison camp in northeastern China. Sometime in September, the woman was flown from Weihsien, China, to a camp in Korea overseen by the U.S. military. It was a location where important American prisoners of war were taken for assessment and preparation prior to returning them to the United States. During this time, Cardinal Spellman attended a meeting in Japan with Lieutenant Colonel Tex McCrary and Jackie Cochran. Speculation was that the three were making arrangements for the repatriation of the unidentified woman.

Though never verified, it has been related that the unidentified woman was disguised as a nun and flown to Japan and then on to the United States. According to researcher Dean Magley, the U.S. government was well aware that the rescued woman was Amelia Earhart. While in Japan, she adopted, or was given, the name Irene Craigmile. With the assistance of the U.S. military and the Catholic Church, "Craigmile" was flown to Rumson, New Jersey, where she was ensconced in an estate owned by Monsignor Kelley.

The selection of the name "Irene Craigmile" was indeed curious. A woman named Irene Craigmile was, in fact, a contemporary of Earhart's, a pilot, and at the time resided in New Jersey.

Prevailing wisdom has Kelley, the good friend of Cardinal Spellman, assisting in the repatriation of Earhart under her new identity and having a hand in helping her recover from her total of eight years of imprisonment and ill treatment at the hands of the Japanese.

According to revelations made by Kelley during the 1980s, he admitted to having had a role in the repatriation and rehabilitation of Amelia Earhart. He stated to Helen Barber, one of his neighbors on the island of St. Croix, that he was enlisted to help bring Earhart back from Japan and that he was chosen to serve as her "psychiatric priest." For the time that Earhart lived at Kelley's estate, he claimed, he "was able to give her spiritual, emotional, and psychological help." Kelley also told Barber that it was Cardinal Spellman who suggested him as the ideal person to rehabilitate Earhart.

According to Kelley, Earhart told him about a safe-deposit box in New Jersey wherein her birth certificate and other important papers were stored but was "adamant that she no longer wanted to be identified as Amelia Earhart." She never provided Kelley a reason for her decision, but she was inflexible in her demand.

Some have ventured the opinion that Earhart was so humiliated and embarrassed by her forced role as Tokyo Rose that she chose not to return to her former identity. It has also been suggested that if, as has been purported, she was involved in the design and testing of Japanese aircraft and, according to a State Department document, applied for Japanese citizenship, then such things would have been difficult to explain and harder to live down if she were repatriated under her real name.

The notion has also been advanced that Earhart was encouraged by government officials to return to the United States under another identity in order not to embarrass those involved in the flight-around-the-world spy mission, which included Franklin D. Roosevelt and a number of his appointees.

Still others suggested that the eight years as a prisoner of the Japanese, often under terrible conditions, had such an effect on her mind that she opted for what today would be termed a witness protection program. This would have exposed her to a minimum of attention and possible attack from those who would perceive her as a traitor.

Author Joe Klaas expressed the belief that Earhart was "so fed up with the extravagant curiosity of the world and the intrusions of the autograph hunters and with a publicity-minded husband that she agreed to perform espionage for her country in exchange for the permanent peace and privacy of assumed death." Monsignor Kelley stated, "After all she'd been through, she didn't want to be Amelia Earhart anymore."

While under the care of Kelley, Earhart was in regular contact with U.S. government officials who were assisting her with her new identity. The principal motivation for the U.S. government to become involved in "such a complex and difficult operation as the transformation of the identity of Amelia Earhart . . . was embarrassment." The potential for embarrassment to the highest political office in the land was great. The political implications of the knowledge that Earhart had been a prisoner of the Japanese and had been moved through a succession of prison camps were immense. Roosevelt would have been branded as a coward and an incompetent. His image would not have survived such an assault. Thus, it was in the best interest of the U.S. government and Amelia Earhart for her to return under an assumed identity.

In 1991, Earhart researcher Rollin C. Reineck contacted Donald DeKoster, a Detroit resident and good friend of Monsignor Kelley. DeKoster admitted that he and Kelley had had several conversations about Amelia Earhart over the years. He related that the aviatrix had "survived the war, but that she did not retain her identity." DeKoster said that Kelley told him that Earhart did not want to be connected with the Tokyo Rose disgrace along with other issues related to her flight and disappearance. He also stated that her new name was Irene Craigmile.

Kelley passed away in 1996 at the age of ninety-four. Following his passing, permission was granted to Reineck to examine his personal files. Though there were file cabinets and boxes filled with a variety of materials, Reineck found only three Earhart-related items. One was a folder that had the name Amelia Earhart printed on one side and the name Irene Bolam on the other. (Irene Craigmile married Guy Bolam in 1958.) The second item was a handwritten note by Kelley that said, "It's too bad that her mother never knew she had survived."

The third item was a copy of a letter written by the monsignor to Irene Bolam. A portion of the missive contained the following curious passage:

> But by far the most distressing part of this past week was the most terrible treatment you received when leaving. I can never forgive him for simply dropping you off at the airport and then not calling me until 4:00 PM on Sunday. Had I known your high priority was not being recognized by the counter clerk, I would have called the airport manager immediately. It so happens he was upstairs in his office, just above the ticket counter all day Sunday. Our little friend should have used his intelligence and gone up to see him. There would have been no problem. I have since been assured by the manager's secretary. God love and bless you.

From the accumulated evidence, it is clear that Monsignor Kelley was acquainted with Amelia Earhart and Irene Craigmile Bolam and that the two could have been one and the same. It is also clear, based on the previous letter passage, that some level of secrecy relative to Bolam's identity was important.

· 37 ·

Enter Irene Craigmile Bolam

$\mathcal{J}$oe Gervais was a retired command pilot for the U.S. Air Force. He also manifested a deep and enthusiastic passion for all things Amelia Earhart. Gervais was a tireless researcher and spent tens of thousands of dollars of his own money flying to various Pacific islands and interviewing anyone and everyone who might have some connection to Earhart and/or her plane. His name is well known among Earhart enthusiasts, and his passion for studying her disappearance was all consuming. Some critics of Gervais maintain he was too passionate and that he oriented his conclusions to fit predetermined objectives. Regardless, his contributions to the realm of Earhart research cannot be denied.

Following an Earhart research–related visit to Truk Lagoon during the spring of 1965, Gervais arrived home to find in the mail an invitation to speak about his findings to the Early Fliers Club at West Hampton Air Force Base on Sunday, August 8, 1965. The invitation also mentioned that members of the Ninety-Nines would be in attendance. The Ninety-Nines was a women's flying organization; its first president was Amelia Earhart.

Gervais and his wife arrived at a reception held at the Sea Spray Inn on the Dunes, East Hampton, Long Island, New York, on August 8. Three hundred people were in attendance. A large percentage of the members were elderly and had not flown for thirty years or more, but their enthusiasm for aviation had not dimmed with the passage of time.

Gervais was introduced to most of the members. Many of them, he learned, had known Amelia Earhart. As Gervais took photographs of some of these aviation pioneers, Viola Gentry, who had arranged for his visit, was standing nearby. At one point, Gentry glanced about the reception room. Suddenly, according to Gervais, Gentry's "eyes widened and she gasped."

Gentry pointed to a woman in the room and, speaking in a somewhat reverential tone, identified her as Irene Bolam. Gervais turned to look and spotted a "distinguished-appearing, silver haired . . . woman who had just entered the room." Gervais stared at the woman and later stated that at that point he experienced a chill and a slight tremble, for he felt as though he were looking at Amelia Earhart. (Earhart would have been sixty-eight years old in 1965.) Gervais, who had been steeped in Earhartiana for so many years, had a feeling he was looking into the face of the famed aviatrix, "the same face twenty-eight years older than in her last pictures." Her hair was "shaped the same way, short around the head . . . parted the same way." He asked Gentry whether she could arrange for an introduction.

Gentry led Gervais across the room and introduced him to Mr. and Mrs. Guy Bolam. Following the exchange of opening pleasantries, Gervais asked Mrs. Bolam whether she had been a friend of Amelia Earhart. Mrs. Bolam "smiled to a far-off memory" and replied that she knew Earhart.

During the conversation, Gervais noted that hanging around Mrs. Bolam's neck was a silver medallion and pinned to her dress were a miniature major's oak-leaf insignia and a miniature metal replica of the red, white, and blue ribbon which is worn only by winners of the American Distinguished Flying Cross.

Gervais asked Mrs. Bolam whether she was a pilot, and she replied in the affirmative. He asked her whether she ever flew with Earhart, and she said that she had. Nervous and unsure how to proceed with his questioning of Mrs. Bolam, Gervais turned toward Mr. Bolam, who was from England, and asked him what business he was in. Bolam replied that he was in communications. More conversation ensued, during which Gervais elicited the response from Mrs. Bolam that she and Amelia Earhart had flown "together quite a bit."

Unsure about how to continue his questioning, Gervais asked Mrs. Bolam whether she would provide her address so that he might write to her sometime in the future. She glanced at her husband, whose "eyebrows lifted just a touch." Finally, he shrugged and acquiesced. Mrs. Bolam withdrew a card from her purse, wrote something on it, and handed it to Gervais.

Then Gervais held up the camera he was carrying and inquired whether he could take a photograph. Mrs. Bolam demurred and glanced at her husband. Mr. Bolam appeared concerned, hesitated, and said, "I don't know . . ." Before he could finish the sentence, however, Gervais snapped the shutter. Mrs. Bolam appeared quite uncomfortable, and Gentry looked concerned.

Gervais turned to Mrs. Bolam and asked her whether she was a member of the Ninety-Nines. She said she was. When he inquired whether she was a member of the Zontas, the feminist sorority that Earhart had belonged to, she replied that she was. At this point, Guy Bolam interrupted and led his wife away. Gervais turned to Gentry and asked her to confirm that Mrs. Bolam was a member of both the Ninety-Nines and Zontas. Gentry replied that she was.

Gentry excused herself to tend to other guests and left Gervais to mingle with the crowd. That afternoon, Gervais presented his talk to the Early Flyers Club. It dealt with his expedition to Truk Lagoon. During the presentation, he noticed that Mr. and Mrs. Bolam were not present—they had departed the premises. Following Gervais's talk, there ensued a short ceremony wherein his wife, Thelma, was presented the Amelia Earhart Award for Outstanding Contribution to Research in the History of Aviation. The award was presented to her for her assistance to her husband in his ongoing research into Amelia Earhart. The award was a bronze replica of a silver medallion that had once been awarded to Earhart by the city of New York following her first successful flight across the Atlantic Ocean. Gervais noticed that the medal hanging around his wife's neck was the same as one of those he had seen earlier hanging around the neck of Mrs. Bolam.

That evening, Gervais and his wife returned to their room at the Sea Spray Inn. Shortly after arriving, Gervais received a phone call from Mrs. Bolam, who invited him and his wife to join her and her husband at their home for dinner the following evening. She expressed a desire to speak with him about his research into Earhart. As Gervais had already made plans to fly out the next afternoon, he explained and made his apologies. Mrs. Bolam told Gervais that she "would very much like to talk to you," and the disappointment in her voice was manifest. Gervais asked her what she wanted to discuss, and she replied she wanted to talk about his "investigation into Amelia Earhart's disappearance." Gervais, again offering apologies, asked whether he could return another time. Mrs. Bolam told him to come and visit her the next time he came to New York.

Before hanging up, Gervais asked Mrs. Bolam whether she believed Amelia Earhart was dead. She replied, "I believe Amelia Earhart will live as long as people remember her."

Gervais returned home and eventually to his Earhart research. On a hunch, he wrote letters to Zonta International and to the Ninety-Nines, two organizations in which Earhart had been visible and active. He inquired about the claimed membership of Mrs. Bolam. In the process he learned that Irene Bolam's name prior to marrying her current husband was Irene Craigmile. Both groups responded with past and present membership lists. No one named Irene Bolam, Mrs. Guy Bolam, or Irene Craigmile had ever been a member of either organization. Furthermore, subsequent research has revealed that while Earhart and the original Irene Craigmile may possibly have met in the past, the truth is, they had not "flown together quite a bit."

In June 1967, Gervais, while on a trip to New York, attempted to arrange another visit with Irene Bolam. He called the number she had provided him but received no answer. He drove to the address in Bedford Village, but it was clear the house had been unoccupied for some time.

Gervais went to the home of a next-door neighbor and inquired about the Bolams. The neighbor, Mrs. Rakow, said she barely knew Guy Bolam and only saw him when he picked up his mail at the box near the curb. When Gervais asked her whether she knew Mrs. Bolam, Rakow responded with surprise and explained that she was unaware that Mr. Bolam was married.

Gervais called the phone number of Guy Bolam Associates, Inc. in New York City. The information was on the card Mrs. Bolam gave him at the meeting of the Early Flyers Club. He received no answer. Gervais asked a friend who lived in the city to obtain some information about Bolam Associates. The friend replied that the company was apparently involved with some kind of financial or investment activity but was not listed with the Securities and Exchange Commission.

Gervais decided to visit the office of Guy Bolam Associates. It turned out to be part of a suite of several offices that shared a common receptionist. When asked, the receptionist stated she knew absolutely nothing about Guy Bolam Associates and that the suite had been empty since she had worked there.

Gervais went to each of the offices to see whether anyone knew anything about GBA. Most of the offices had been assigned to a variety of foreign legations. The secretary at the Icelandic mission told Gervais she might be able to help him. She said she was acquainted with a Mrs. Burger, who was Bolam's secretary. She provided Gervais with a phone number for Burger.

It was later learned that Guy Bolam once claimed to have been employed by Amalgamated Telephone and Telegraph. When contacted, however, AT&T said they had never heard of him. In addition, the British-born Bolam has been linked to the Council on Foreign Relations and may have once served as an agent for MI6, the British equivalent of the Central Intelligence Agency. The presence of Guy Bolam in the Amelia Earhart saga adds yet another layer of mystery, and it remains odd how such a man possessing a somewhat impressive, perhaps distinguished, as well as clandestine background of some level of national importance became associated with Irene Craigmile, who was identified as a "typical middle class housewife with a less than impressive flying record."

Gervais dialed the number that was answered by Burger. He asked for Guy Bolam. Burger said Bolam was in Europe on business and would not return for ten days. When he inquired about Mrs. Bolam, Burger said she was "staying at the residence of her nurse and companion, Peggy Salter, in

Sanford, North Carolina." Burger provided the telephone number in North Carolina. Burger explained that Mrs. Bolam had been suffering from shingles.

When Gervais called the North Carolina number, Mrs. Bolam answered. Following a few minutes of small talk, Gervais told Bolam he would like to visit with her "about the old days and Amelia Earhart." Bolam replied, "Oh, I can't see you in this country. If I meet with you at all it can't be in this country." As Gervais was puzzling over this rather odd statement, Bolam went on to explain that she had once had a career in flying and an accompanying public life and that she had removed herself from all of that now. The truth is, the real Irene Craigmile never had a career in flying, nor had she an accompanying public life.

Finally, Gervais was able to make arrangements for the two of them to meet on June 23 at 7:00 p.m. in the lobby of the Laurentian Hotel in Montreal. Gervais began making plans for the trip, anticipating that at long last he would learn the truth about Irene Craigmile Bolam.

· 38 ·

Enter William Van Dusen

$\mathcal{I}$n the evening following his telephone conversation with Mrs. Bolam, Gervais made arrangements to have dinner with a man named William Van Dusen at his home. During his earlier research of Earhart, Gervais had encountered Van Dusen's name and was curious to see whether he could shed some light on the Earhart/Bolam mystery. As it turned out, Van Dusen, who at the time was a vice president with Eastern Airlines, established contact with Gervais. Specifically, Van Dusen expressed curiosity about what kind of information Gervais had uncovered regarding his research on Amelia Earhart.

During the meal, Van Dusen said to Gervais that he had heard he was going to Montreal in the morning. Surprised, Gervais asked him how he could possibly know such a thing since the only other person who was aware of his plans was Irene Craigmile Bolam. Van Dusen didn't answer, only smiled. During their conversation, Gervais was struck by what he regarded as an uncanny resemblance between Van Dusen and Fred Noonan. At one point, Van Dusen mentioned that he and Earhart had been good friends. When Gervais attempted to probe the depth and kind of friendship, Van Dusen "adroitly changed the subject without really answering the question."

At another point during the conversation, Van Dusen's wife said to him, "Why don't you tell Major Gervais what he wants to know?" For a moment, Van Dusen's mood darkened and he aimed a strong comment at his wife. With the passage of another minute, he had regained his composure and resumed the conversation with Gervais but continued to be evasive about Fred Noonan.

During the conversation, Van Dusen produced a silver cigarette case and offered Gervais a smoke. Gervais declined, and when Van Dusen placed one in his own mouth, Gervais noticed that the inscription on the case was

142

to Fred Noonan for his service to Pan American Airlines. When Gervais asked his host where he had obtained the cigarette case, Van Dusen replied, enigmatically, that "Fred must have left it here or something." When Gervais pressed for information on the cigarette case, Van Dusen once again changed the subject.

The above is a telling encounter. When could Fred Noonan, who disappeared nearly three decades earlier, possibly have left a cigarette lighter at the home of Van Dusen? Further, there exists no information relative to the notion that the two men had ever met, much less that they were friends. Unless, of course, Van Dusen was Noonan.

Later, when Gervais was leaving the Van Dusen residence, he looked back to wave and saw his host standing next to his wife. His pose and posture, according to Gervais, was exactly like what he had seen in a photo of Fred Noonan.

Gervais had done some background checking on Van Dusen. He learned that, according to information released by Van Dusen himself, he was born in Toledo, Ohio. Later, when Gervais initiated a search for a birth certificate, however, none was to be found. Nor was Fred Noonan's.

· 39 ·

Reenter Irene Craigmile Bolam

$\mathcal{O}$n the afternoon following his conversation with William Van Dusen, Joe Gervais arrived at the Laurentian Hotel and asked the desk clerk whether a Mrs. Guy Bolam was registered. He replied that she had a reservation but had not checked in yet. Gervais signed in for his room and decided to wait in the lobby for the arrival of Mrs. Bolam. He waited for hours. Finally, at 1:00 a.m. the next morning, he gave up and went to his room. At sunrise, he called down to the desk to find out whether Bolam had arrived. She had not.

After waiting for twenty-four hours, Gervais finally caught a plane back to New York. He had Bolam paged every hour at the Laurentian and called the Bolam telephone number in Princeton, New Jersey, as well as those in New York City and North Carolina. No answers. In desperation, he called the secretary, Helen Burger, again to inquire whether she had any current information. Burger expressed surprise that Bolam did not make the Montreal appointment and told Gervais that she was still in North Carolina waiting for Mr. Bolam to return from Europe.

Gervais called the North Carolina number again. Peggy Salter answered and told him that Mrs. Bolam could not come to the phone, explaining that she was ill. When Gervais insisted, Salter grew irritated, told him not to call anymore, and hung up. He called Burger back and requested that she have Guy Bolam call him on his return from Europe.

Several days later, Guy Bolam, who had returned to New York, called Gervais. He seemed not to be bothered at all when Gervais explained how Mrs. Bolam stood him up in Montreal and extended an invitation for Gervais to fly to North Carolina on June 29 and meet with Mrs. Bolam then. They agreed to meet at the Newark Airport for the 4:00 p.m. flight to Raleigh.

Gervais checked with the airline to see whether Guy Bolam did, in fact, have a reservation. The clerk assured him that he did. When the plane lifted off on the afternoon of June 29, however, Guy Bolam was not on board.

At Raleigh, Gervais rented a car and drove to the Sanford address forty miles away. A gardener working in the yard informed him that a short time earlier the Bolams had loaded their luggage into a vehicle and driven away. He did not know their destination.

Two days later Gervais called Burger again for information on the whereabouts of Mr. and Mrs. Guy Bolam. She had no information for him but suggested he try the Bolam's Jamesburg residence and gave him a phone number. When Gervais called, Mrs. Bolam answered and demanded to know where he got the number. Gervais explained his problems related to keeping appointments with her and her husband. She asked him why he was going to all of this trouble to talk with her and he told her he wanted to visit with her about her early days of flying. She replied that she had "left all that." After more discussion, Bolam told Gervais to "put exactly what you want from me in writing and send it to me. If I want to discuss it with you I may invite you to lunch at the Wings Club."

With the assistance of fellow researcher and author Joe Klaas, Gervais drafted a multipage letter in which he explained that he kept "turning up facts which indicate that Amelia Earhart is alive" and stated that he believed it was possible that she, Irene Bolam, was Amelia Earhart. He stated, in fact, that he was trying everything in his power to prove she was *not* Earhart but that it was difficult. He requested background information from Mrs. Bolam to assist him in proving that she was not the aviatrix.

Bolam replied two weeks later. She provided Gervais with the names of two individuals who could verify that Amelia Earhart and Irene Bolam were two different people: Viola Gentry and Elmo Neale Pickerill. Gervais was suspicious. He had met both Gentry and Pickerill at the same gathering where he met Irene Bolam, at the Early Flyers Club on Long Island. He was aware that both were close friends of Bolam and suspected they would do anything she asked of them. He wrote anyway. Gentry responded that Irene's maiden name was O'Crowley, that she had married a man named Craigmile, was widowed, and then married Guy Bolam. Pickerill said he had known Mrs. Bolam for thirty years. In between the death of Mr. Craigmile and the wedding to Bolam, he said, Irene married Al Heller, and the two had a son. Irene, he said, learned to fly under the instruction of Heller.

Gervais submitted requests to the Department of Transportation, Federal Aviation Commission, in Oklahoma City seeking information about pilot licenses issued to Amelia Earhart, Viola Gentry, Jacqueline (Cochran) Odlum, Irene Heller, and Irene Craigmile.

The response from Eddie H. Kjelshus, Chief of Airman Certification Branch, Flight Standards Technical Division, revealed that no license was ever issued to an Irene Heller but that a private license, number 28958, had been issued to an Irene Craigmile on May 27, 1933.

Gervais decided to obtain a copy of Irene Craigmile's pilot's license. He received one: license number 28958, issued to Irene O. Craigmile, age 31. The license was unsigned, in contrast with the information provided by the FAC, and dated May 31, 1937. To further complicate matters, that date was crossed out, and penciled above it was June 1, 1937. The address on the license was Brooklyn, New York. Not only did it not contain Craigmile's signature, the required signature of an officer of the Bureau of Air Commerce was nowhere present. The unsigned license had been placed in the files and was never picked up. If someone named Irene Craigmile ever flew an airplane, she did so without a license.

Technically, then, there was no evidence whatsoever that a license had been provided to Irene Craigmile in 1933 as indicated in the earlier response from the FAA. June 1, 1937, incidentally, was the day Amelia Earhart took off from Miami, Florida, on her attempt to fly around the world. Coincidence? Author Joe Klaas advanced the question: Did Irene Craigmile/O'Crowley/Heller/Bolam begin to exist only as Amelia Earhart set out on her journey?

Gervais and Klaas collaborated on another letter to Mrs. Bolam. In it, they explained that they were working on a book that was intended to tell the true story of Amelia Earhart. He asked for her "indulgence in helping us prove beyond a shadow of a doubt that you are *not* indeed she." Gervais stressed to Mrs. Bolam that he wanted to give her "every opportunity to clear up any mistakes at all we might be making."

There was no response to the letter. Later, Viola Gentry visited Gervais and informed him that Mrs. Bolam had departed for Paris and that he would never see her again. During their conversation, Gervais told Gentry that "there were a lot of people interested in this case . . . and that it would be worth a lot of money to find out what really happened . . . on July 2, 1937." In an odd reply, Gentry said, "That's what Amelia says."

If the woman going by the name Irene Craigmile Bolam was not Amelia Earhart, it would have been a simple and uncomplicated matter to meet briefly with Major Gervais and provide him with the pertinent documentation. Instead, Mrs. Bolam remained evasive, inconsistent, and contradictory, thus providing reasons for suspicion. She went to great lengths to avoid meeting with the researcher. Gervais's research appeared in the book *Amelia Earhart Lives*, authored by Joe Klaas. Published by McGraw-Hill, it was released in 1970. In it, Klaas provided for the possibility that Irene Craigmile Bolam and Amelia Earhart were the same person.

Robert Myers was the young boy befriended by Amelia Earhart at Oakland Airport as she was preparing for her around-the-world flight. Myers had no connection to or association with Joe Gervais whatsoever. Independent of Gervais's contention that he discovered Amelia Earhart in the form of Irene Craigmile Bolam, Robert Myers also made a startling discovery. As an adult, Myers went to see a film in a downtown Oakland, California, movie theater. As he watched and was only half-listening to the Movietone newsreel, he was shocked to see a woman he was convinced was Amelia Earhart. Her looks, her voice, her mannerisms, and even her comments were similar. The news clip showed Irene Craigmile Bolam standing at a podium during a press conference and denying that she was the famous aviatrix. In spite of that, Myers said, "I knew it was Amelia. She looked like Amelia. She even sounded like Amelia. I knew it was [her]."

Curious about a number of aspects relative to the so-called disappearance of Amelia Earhart and the appearance of Irene Craigmile Bolam, Myers decided to seek some answers. He wrote a letter to Mrs. Bolam but never received a reply. He decided he would call her and obtained her phone number from directory assistance. According to Myers, the moment Bolam answered the telephone, he was convinced she was Amelia Earhart. Myers taped all of his subsequent calls to Bolam.

"I thought she sounded like Amelia," wrote Myers. "Her voice mannerisms were the same. In these phone calls, and there were several, she listened to me, she cried, expressed recognition of what I told her, and generally spoke to me in such a way as to convince me that I was really talking to Amelia."

At one point during one of the conversations, Bolam told Myers, "I have said openly that I am not Amelia. I was just wondering what you know. . . . Today you wonder whether there's anything else someone wants you to do."

When Myers discussed the disappearance of Earhart with Bolam, she stated, "It's very difficult to imagine what I went through . . . because you have to live through the damn thing!" When the subject of George Palmer Putnam came up, Bolam, her ire rising, said, "He got his! He paid for what he did to me!" According to Myers, he and Irene Craigmile Bolam communicated by telephone off and on for almost four years.

Myers was determined to meet with Irene Craigmile Bolam face to face. An arrangement was made to rendezvous on a public street corner in New Jersey. Bolam arrived in a chauffer-driven automobile that parked near where Myers was standing. After instructing the driver to leave the vehicle for a time, she lowered her window and invited Myers to come closer.

Myers wrote, "When I saw her, there was no doubt in my mind that I was looking at Amelia Earhart. She had changed. She seemed much older and hardened . . . [but she] still had mannerisms of her younger years. Her patterns of speech had not changed and many of her words convinced me."

When Myers related to Bolam the incident where George Palmer Putnam attempted to hit him with his car, she replied, "Why didn't you tell me? I could have done something about it then."

Before they parted, Bolam said to Myers, "You know I cannot help you. I cannot tell you that I am Amelia Earhart, but I want you to know the things you say are all true."

Even without the connections to Amelia Earhart established by Gervais and Myers, the life of Irene Craigmile Bolam itself invites suspicion and a number of questions. For example, Bolam moved throughout aviation circles and received what could only be described as deferential treatment by all. During the late 1960s, Bolam was presented an award by NASA. Given her rather unimpressive flying record—less than one year of lessons and flying time—this seems odd. Though she claimed to be an ordinary housewife, Bolam, in truth, associated with a number of influential people and was close to many in the higher echelons of government and flying. Author Gervais, however, on researching the early days of women flyers in the United States, found no references to Irene Craigmile Bolam at all.

Irene Craigmile Bolam passed away on July 7, 1982. Her age was listed as seventy-eight. According to a 1982 article in the Woodbridge, New Jersey, *News Tribune*, Bolam's personal physician, Dr. Man Wah Cheung, "remained puzzled about [her], even after her death, and wasn't so sure she was not Amelia Earhart."

The same article also points out that several members of the Wings Club, described as "an exclusive aviators' organization in New York City," were quoted as having suspicions that Bolam was indeed Amelia Earhart, based on her uncanny resemblance to the aviatrix and the occasional strange remarks she made."

Diana Dawes was a longtime friend of Irene Bolam. Dawes described Bolam as "a very mysterious lady." Dawes was quoted as saying that there were a number of odd things that Bolam said "that indicated she was Amelia Earhart."

In another Woodbridge *News Tribune* article, a man named John Malloy related the substance of a conversation he once had with Bolam. She told him, "In all the years I flew, I never wore a parachute." Irene Bolam's entire flight record covers only six months from late 1932 to early 1933. It is not possible that she had flown for years.

During one of Bolam's conversations with author Joe Gervais, she stated, "I once had a public life. I once had a career in flying, but I've retired. I've given all that up now." Such a comment could not have possibly come from a person with Irene Bolam's aviation background, for she had no career in flying whatsoever, nor did she ever have much of a public life. Such a comment, however, could have legitimately come from someone such as Amelia Earhart.

Both Bolam's brother-in-law and sister-in-law were quoted as stating that she was not the person she presented herself to be. The brother-in-law was quoted as saying that he was not convinced that she was who she claimed to be. Even the purported son of the original Irene Craigmile, Larry Heller, along with his wife, Joan, questioned his mother's true identity. Heller even attempted to obtain the fingerprints of Irene Craigmile Bolam after she died but was denied.

Irene Craigmile Bolam was, for the most part, a reclusive woman who appeared in public on rare occasions, most of them being associated with aviation organizations.

Evidence of an interesting coincidence has surfaced. During a time period from 1932 to 1933, Earhart, Irene Craigmile, Jackie Cochran, and Viola Gentry, all female flyers, flew in and out of Roosevelt Field, New York, as well as nearby Bennett Field. It is difficult to believe that these four women did not know each other.

In another interesting account provided by Myers, a friend of Irene Craigmile Bolam took a photograph of her to a psychic for a response. The event took place several weeks after Bolam had passed way. Myers provided the psychic no information on the identity of the person in the photograph or any of the circumstances pertaining to his relationship with Earhart. After considering the image for several minutes, the psychic said, "This woman did not die of natural causes; it will appear as though she did. The woman is terrified and has been living in fear for years. She knows a lot of people, and I see dirty politics around this woman."

During the time Robert Myers was active in researching Amelia Earhart and discussing the Earhart-Bolam connection, he received telephone calls from an unknown person or persons threatening him with death if he did not "keep your mouth shut about Earhart." The exact source of the calls remains a mystery, but in the end, the only people who could have been hurt or embarrassed by Myers's revelations would have been politicians and other elected and appointed government officials, past and present.

And there is this: If Irene Craigmile Bolam was not Amelia Earhart, one must wonder why she agreed to telephone conversations with Myers over a period of four years.

Irene Rutherford O'Crowley, the aunt of a woman identified as Irene Craigmile Bolam, served as Earhart's attorney during the early 1930s. She claimed she was introduced to Earhart in Europe following the aviatrix's first solo flight across the Atlantic. A coincidence?

And there is this mystery. Author Rollin Reineck discovered that Irene Craigmile Bolam's brother and sister-in-law donated an engraved brick to the Amelia Earhart Museum in Atchison, Kansas. The brick was placed in the walkway that led to the front door of Earhart's childhood home and bore the somewhat cryptic engraving: "Irene E. Bolam in memory of Irene C. Bolam."

· 40 ·

Postrepatriation

$\mathscr{A}$s Amelia Earhart, a.k.a. Irene Craigmile Bolam, reentered the world and society following her repatriation and rehabilitation, she skirted the edges of previous levels of celebrity and recognition she once enjoyed, all of which stopped short of allowing for her to become a public figure again. She counted among her friends Senator Barry Goldwater, Justice Anthony Kennedy, and others. She was often seen in the company of well-known aviators, including a number of individuals known to have been close to Earhart during the 1930s. With the passage of time, it became clear to a body of Earhart researchers that there were several people who were well aware that Irene Craigmile Bolam was, in fact, the famous aviatrix but kept the knowledge of her identity to themselves. Author Joe Klaas writes, "The closer you get to friends and family of Amelia Earhart, the more you feel a conspiracy of silence."

During conversations with acquaintances, Irene Craigmile Bolam stated she knew Wiley Post and other famous aviators of the time. She was quite intimate with topics related to aircraft and flying, with instruments, and with airports around the world. Given Irene Craigmile Bolam's actual flying record, such information would have been difficult to impossible to come by.

Earhart married Guy Bolam in 1958 and settled into a home in Bedford Hills, New York. Both were in their fifties. Bolam was born in England, and at the time of their marriage he worked for Radio Luxembourg. How they met has never been clarified. It has always been a matter of curiosity to a number of Earhart researchers how and why Irene Craigmile Bolam, along with her husband, were regarded so highly at gatherings of famous pilots when, in fact, the real Irene Bolam had few, if any, credentials. Amelia Earhart, on the other hand, had them in abundance.

151

Here is another curious truth. By the time Joe Gervais advanced the possibility of Irene Craigmile Bolam being Amelia Earhart and undertook a spate of research and investigation in an attempt to prove such, it was discovered that no family photographs of the original Irene O'Crowley, as well as documents relating to personal history, existed prior to 1940. School attendance records "existed in sketchy form." Allegedly, she graduated from Barringer High School in New Jersey, but there is no record of her graduation, nor does a photograph of her appear in the school annual. In addition, her birth certificate was never found.

There is more. It was discovered that Irene O'Crowley had been engaged to a physician for a short time, but the relationship eventually dissolved. She subsequently became engaged to Charles Craigmile, a civil engineer. Prior to their courtship, however, Irene became pregnant by another man. She gave birth to the child, who was then adopted by her childless uncle, Clarence, and his wife, Violet. The child was named Clarence Rutherford O'Crowley Jr. His illegitimate birth was a well-kept family secret for years but was finally acknowledged by relatives.

In 1924, another child, a girl, arrived on the scene. Initially, she was taken in by the attorney Irene O'Crowley. Attorney Irene, as well as Earhart publicist Nina Price, were close friends with Amelia as well as being business partners. Attorney Irene advised on business matters, and Price assisted Amelia in launching her clothing and luggage products. The girl, as with the earlier boy, eventually went to live with Clarence O'Crowley. No living O'Crowley descendant is certain of the origin of the child, and the relationship remains controversial. A story surfaced a short time after her arrival, however, that the baby girl had been born out of wedlock to Amelia Earhart. The birth was kept secret from the public, but a rumor persisted that the aviatrix bore an illegitimate child at the age of thirty. The child grew up known as "Irene Jr." Photographs of Irene Jr. reveal that she looks remarkably like Amelia Earhart.

Irene Jr. was eventually relocated in Scotland. In time, she had a child herself. Irene Craigmile Bolam, a.k.a. Amelia Earhart, who was living in Rumson, New Jersey, made a number of trips to Scotland in her later years. During the mid-1960s, a woman named Grace McGuire moved from Scotland to Rumson, New Jersey. Grace, who stated she was born and raised in Scotland, claimed she was adopted. Shortly after arriving in Rumson, the twenty-one-year-old Grace became close friends with the original Irene Craigmile's son, Larry Heller, who was born in 1934. She also spent several years as a friend and traveling companion of Muriel Morrissey, Amelia Earhart's sister. Grace McGuire has been described as "a reincarnated version" of Amelia Earhart.

In an interesting aside, Grace McGuire visited Howland Island, where she was photographed waving two flags. One was the flag of Scotland, and the other was the state flag of Kansas, where Earhart was born. Sometime during the 2000s, Grace obtained a Lockheed Electra Model 10.

Charles O'Crowley passed away in 1931, succumbing to appendicitis. Two years later the original Irene O'Crowley Craigmile married Alvin Victor Heller, who had been giving her flying lessons. Evidence exists that this had been arranged by Amelia Earhart and good friend Viola Gentry.

According to researchers, little to nothing was heard from the original Irene O'Crowley Craigmile after 1934.

· 41 ·

Reenter William Van Dusen

$\mathcal{T}$he revelations concerning Mrs. Irene Craigmile Bolam were puzzling, conflicting, and suspicious, to be sure. As time went by, an undercurrent of communication as well as gossip began linking Irene Craigmile Bolam to Amelia Earhart. Another added layer of mystery, however, can be found in the person of William Van Dusen, whom a number of researchers are convinced was Earhart's navigator, Fred Noonan.

William Van Dusen, even in his old age, bore a striking resemblance to Noonan. It had been remarked on several occasions that Van Dusen's posture and manner of walking was identical to that of the navigator. Author David K. Bowman stated that when one compares photos of Noonan and Van Dusen, the faces appear to be "not just similar . . . [but] identical, down to their distinctive sharp noses and the deep creases at either sides of their mouths." William Van Dusen appears for all the world to look like an elderly Fred Noonan.

In what may be little more than a curious coincidence, it was pointed out that Fred Noonan was fond of wearing polka-dot neckties. Oddly, William Van Dusen's preferred style of necktie was also those with polka-dots.

While a great deal of attention has been provided to the notion that Amelia Earhart did survive her alleged government-endorsed demise in the Pacific Ocean and returned, little notice has been given to the possibility that the same can be said for Fred Noonan. As it turns out, Noonan has been much harder to track than Earhart. Following his internment on the island of Saipan, little to nothing is known of his fate or whereabouts.

Fred Noonan was legally declared dead in 1938. Between 1939 and 1940, a man named William Van Dusen was suddenly and heavily involved with transatlantic and South Pacific flights, a role previously assumed by

Noonan. In fact, Van Dusen has been credited with "pioneering" such flights. This credit had previously been applied to Fred Noonan. Van Dusen was also closely acquainted with Charles Lindbergh and other noted pilots of the day.

A search for Fred Noonan's birth certificate by researcher/author Gervais revealed none on file. Furthermore, a search for Noonan's personnel records at Pan American Airways resulted in the determination that none could be located. Consider this: at one time Fred Noonan was hailed as Pan Am's most distinguished trailblazing navigator, was regarded by his peers as the most skilled navigator in the country, and was involved in the most famous disappearance and mystery of the century. Yet the company he was associated with possessed not a single record. Van Dusen, however, had an extensive file.

It gets even more bizarre. It has long been standard procedure for members of the U.S. armed forces to be fingerprinted on enlistment. Noonan held the rank of lieutenant commander in the United States Naval Reserve, yet there are no fingerprints on file for him.

For William Van Dusen, allegedly born in Toledo, Ohio, there is likewise no birth certificate. Author Gervais learned that when Van Dusen learned of Gervais's investigations into the disappearance of Amelia Earhart, he immediately contacted the U.S. Air Force and Coast Guard as well as the National Archives in an attempt to learn what Gervais had discovered. When Gervais submitted a request to Pan American Airways in Los Angeles for information about Fred Noonan, the company's historian referred him to William Van Dusen.

On one occasion when Gervais was interviewing Van Dusen, he told him that he had learned the elderly man had had a profile search conducted on him. Gervais informed Van Dusen that he likewise ran a search on him and discovered there was no birth certificate on file at the location Van Dusen claimed. Van Dusen responded, "Sometimes I do have a little trouble proving who I am."

If Van Dusen had told the truth about his identity, then why would proving it present a problem? The truth is, this kind of information gathering is cut and dried and normally presents few, if any, problems. Unless, of course, one is lying.

· 42 ·

The Evidence

$\mathscr{A}$ccording to author Thomas E. Devine, the U.S. government "holds 113 sealed documents pertaining to the Earhart case." Devine advances the notion that these documents are kept from the public in order to cover up the deceptions associated with and the mistakes made relative to the in-flight aid supplied to Earhart as well as the botched search. Others contend that the documents also reveal the fate of Earhart following her landing in the Marshall Islands, her subsequent imprisonment by the Japanese, and what ultimately became of her relative to her hypothesized repatriation to the United States.

There are two schools of thought relative to what happened to Amelia Earhart on July 2, 1937. The U.S. government issued a press release stating that Earhart, along with her navigator Fred Noonan, crashed into the Pacific Ocean near Howland Island and perished. This is the "official" version of what happened. It is also the version that is believed by the majority of people around the world since it is the one that was most commonly seen in newspapers and newsreels at the time. Furthermore, a number of books have been published purporting to tell the true story of the aviatrix but that adhere to the "official," though clearly flawed, version of the event. For many, this position has become firmly established in their consciousness, and few have felt any need to remove it. It should be pointed out that despite being the official and most widely accepted account of what happed to Earhart, it carries with it no substantive evidence whatsoever. Curiously, reams of material related to the disappearance of and search for Amelia Earhart have been categorized as top secret by the U.S. government and made unavailable to researchers. One cannot help but wonder what sort of information the government found necessary to hide from public examination if it had been telling the truth all along.

There exist other schools of thought as they relate to Earhart's fate. The most prevalent alternative explanation relates to the notion that Earhart and Noonan's plane came down near a Japanese-controlled island and that the two were captured, arrested, and subsequently imprisoned by the rulers. While evidence for the first school of thought is lacking or absent, the evidence for the second is abundant and, frankly, difficult to dispute.

As a corollary to theory number two, the notion has been advanced that Earhart, after being freed from a Japanese prison on mainland China, was repatriated to the United States, where she underwent a period of rehabilitation and, for whatever reason, an identity change. A number of Earhart researchers are persuaded that Earhart lived out the rest of her life under the assumed name of Irene Craigmile Bolam.

It is incumbent upon any researcher/investigator to analyze any and all evidence pertinent to the Earhart/Bolam connection relative to making a determination with regard to the truth.

THE PHOTOGRAPHIC ANALYSIS

In an attempt to prove that Irene Craigmile Bolam was Amelia Earhart, a man named Tod Swindell arrived at a technique in 1997 wherein transparent photographic overlays were developed such that, he claimed, the facial features of Earhart and Bolam could be compared. Swindell was a member of the Screen Director's Guild as well as a member of the Amelia Earhart Society. His credentials for conducting a statistically valid photo-analysis technique were nonexistent.

Swindell obtained photographic images of both Earhart and Bolam from a number of sources. He searched for photographs of the two women that shared a common pose. An overlay of one, according to author Rollin Reineck, had to be the same size as the photo of the other. In the final analysis, any significant "problems were overcome," and, according to Swindell, the experiment revealed that the images of Amelia Earhart from the 1930s aligned "precisely" with those of Irene Craigmile Bolam. In Swindell's opinion, as well as that of Reineck, it was a perfect match.

Reineck reported that Swindell "persevered and his tireless efforts have successfully produced outstanding results that are acceptable to the scientific community as proof that Irene Bolam and Amelia Earhart were the same person." Furthermore, Swindell claimed to have done a "forensic analysis on her complete life story." Quite a claim, indeed, though Swindell had no credentials for such an undertaking, and to date it has not been forthcoming.

In his book *Amelia Earhart Survived*, Reineck claims that two forensic anthropologists—Dr. Walter Birkby and Dr. Todd W. Fenton—"fully recognized the Earhart Bolam controversy through the quality of Swindell's extensive physical and personal traits comparisons." "With the enormous amount of research presented to them," according to Reineck, they felt that it was hard to disagree with the conclusion that "Amelia Earhart and Irene Bolam were one and the same."

Reineck goes on to claim that "this was the affirmation needed using forensic science methodology" to determine that Earhart and Bolam were one and the same.

There was a second photo-comparison project involving Earhart and Bolam, this one independently conducted by a man named David Allen Deal and had two pages devoted to it in David Bowman's book, *Legerdemain*. Deal's "technique" involved employing photographic overlays of similar poses and then aligning the overlay/photo match to determine a resemblance or otherwise. Deal concludes his study with the comment, "I cannot see how these photographs can fail to convince a reasonable person."

Swindell and Reineck, as well as Deal, could not have been more mistaken. While there appears to be an impressive array of compelling evidence yielding the strong suggestion that Amelia Earhart did not crash and sink in the Pacific Ocean and that she was returned to the United States under a new identity, the photographic experiments performed by Swindell and Deal have never been accepted by professional photo-comparison experts as part of it. Though Swindell's photographic analysis has been advanced on dozens of occasions to point out the similarities between Earhart and Bolam, it proves absolutely nothing. Likewise, Deal's project was so absurdly amateurish that it is difficult to believe anyone found legitimacy in it. While their conclusions were on target, their methodology was flawed.

Since the 1970s, computers and attendant hardware and software have been available with the capacity to conduct scientifically accurate and statistically valid photo-comparison studies. At least two oft-tested, validated, and statistically proven systems for facial pattern recognition have come into common usage by law enforcement organizations worldwide, including the Central Intelligence Agency, the Federal Bureau of Investigation, Scotland Yard, Interpol, and a number of other local and regional agencies. The most widely employed was developed by Y. Kaya and K. Kobayashi and made available via Academic Press in New York.

These photo-comparison techniques are widely used today, and the results are admissible in court. One such application of one of these scientifically valid systems was employed to make a determination related to whether or not a man named William Henry Roberts, who died in Hamilton County, Texas, in 1949, was actually the famous outlaw Billy the Kid. The results of the study proved that he was (*Billy the Kid: Beyond the Grave*, Taylor Trade Publishing, 2005).

It is therefore puzzling that Swindell and Deal, while having access to legitimate and recognized state-of-the-art photo-analysis techniques in 1997 chose to ignore them and pursue a line of "research" that amounts to little more than a junior high school classroom project. It is important to emphasize that the results arrived at were purely subjective and possessed no statistical validity whatsoever. They must, therefore, be rejected as proof that Amelia Earhart and Irene Craigmile Bolam were the same person.

Amateurish research projects by enthusiasts such as the above have created problems for legitimate researchers and investigators in pursuit of the truth. When opponents of the Amelia Earhart = Irene Craigmile Bolam hypothesis want to make a case for the unprofessional and unskilled nature of the proposals advanced by the other side, they invariably point to the projects conducted by Swindell and Deal, which made a mockery of photo-recognition analysis. The truth is, a legitimate, statistically valid photo analysis has, to date, not been undertaken involving Earhart and Bolam.

Further, Reineck's claim that two "renowned forensic anthropologists . . . felt that it was hard to disagree with" Swindell's conclusions is either a gross exaggeration or a huge error. If the two men had indeed been "renowned," they would have known of the availability of existing statistically valid photo-comparison techniques. One wonders why Reineck regarded the two men as renowned when at that time such unrefined and amateur techniques as applied by Swindell were completely rejected by those in the photo-comparison business. Reineck's use of the term "forensic science methodology" when referring to Swindell's study is completely misleading and untrue.

Based on scientific methodology as well as common sense, the Swindell and Deal photo-comparison projects are completely worthless when trying to establish a connection between Earhart and Irene Craigmile Bolam and do little more than provide ammunition for the proponents of the status quo.

On the other hand, however, there are numerous other aspects of the Earhart-Bolam connection that are conducive to generating suspicion about the true identity of the woman known as Irene Craigmile Bolam.

To compound the problems associated with the connection between Amelia Earhart and the woman named Irene Craigmile Bolam, there have been two different women carrying the Craigmile identity. An article in the Woodbridge, New Jersey, *Times Tribune* showed that photos of a woman identified as Bolam were those of a person different from the one Gervais met at the meeting of the Early Flyers Club.

One author stated that Bolam's height, arm length, hands, and fingers were identical to Earhart's. He also claimed that their handwriting was identical, though this has never been verified. In his 1970 book *Amelia Earhart Lives*, author Joe Klaas credits the source of a great deal of the information he placed in the book as Earhart researcher Joe Gervais. Based on the research at his disposal, Klaas put forth the notion that Irene Craigmile Bolam was likely Amelia Earhart. He did not state that it was an absolute fact but that the evidence could easily lead one to believe they were one and the same woman.

Within days following the release of the book, Mrs. Bolam made arrangements for a news conference that was attended by a number of prominent news agencies of the day. An angry Irene Bolam walked up to the podium and with no opening comments stated that the book was a "cruel hoax." She then slammed the book down on a table and sternly announced, "I am not Amelia Earhart," turned, and walked out.

This seems like an odd, unnecessary, and perhaps overly defensive reaction by Bolam to the publication. In the first place, Klaas never came right out and stated that Bolam was Earhart but only intimated that it was possible. In the second place, Bolam's reaction to the book seemed unusual. Amelia Earhart was, in the minds of virtually every living person on earth, a woman of high accomplishment, a heroine, and an inspiration to many. To be so dramatically upset at being compared with such a noted person seems unwarranted. There was nothing whatsoever negative in the association, nothing insulting. It was, in fact, rather complimentary. Most women, one would think, would be pleased with such an identity.

One week following the Bolam news conference, an odd article appeared in the November 21 issue of *Time* magazine. A portion of it stated:

> The woman they name as Amelia is Mrs. Irene Bolam, widow of a businessman and now living in Monroe Township, New Jersey. She emerged long enough last week to ridicule the book as a poorly documented hoax. Before the press conference was over, the woman from New Jersey had convinced many she was not Amelia Earhart, but some wondered if she were really Mrs. Irene Bolam.

The last line is quite puzzling, but no explanation accompanied it.

For seven weeks following the release of *Amelia Earhart Lives* it was a best seller. Then McGraw-Hill suddenly pulled it from distribution and recalled all copies. Since there was nothing libelous in the publication, the action by McGraw-Hill is curious. Though no details were ever learned, it has been suggested that the move to cease publication and retrieve all copies was ordered by the U.S. government. The book has since been reissued.

Months later, Irene Bolam filed a two-million-dollar lawsuit against author Joe Klaas and researcher Joe Gervais for "invasion of privacy and libel." A definition of libel, according to the *New Lexicon Webster's Dictionary of the English Language*, states, "A published statement, photograph, etc. which without due cause has the result, or is intended to have the result, of bringing its subject into disrepute." A thorough reading of *Amelia Earhart Lives* reveals nothing libelous, scandalous, slanderous, or even remotely negative regarding Mrs. Bolam. If anything, she is depicted as a charming and respected individual.

Five years passed, and the lawsuit was never brought to court. The delays were not the result of action by the defendants but rather by Irene Bolam herself. The defendants—Klaas and Gervais, and presumably McGraw-Hill—were interested in settling the case and expressed a willingness to arrive at a suitable determination if Irene Bolam would provide, in the presence of the judge, her fingerprints in order to prove once and for all that she was not Amelia Earhart. Bolam refused, and her refusal ultimately resulted in the relinquishment of a sizable settlement.

Less than one month later, the suit against Klaas and Gervais was dismissed for "factual errata." One of the errors pointed out was that the book referred to Guy Bolam as her "alleged" husband when in fact they were legally married. McGraw-Hill settled out of court for $60,000. The attorney for McGraw-Hill was convinced that Bolam and Earhart were one and the same but determined it would have been too costly for the publishing company to pursue the case. The only conclusion that can be arrived at is that Irene Craigmile Bolam did not wish her true identity a matter of legal record.

Irene Craigmile Bolam passed away on July 7, 1982. According to stipulations in her will, her body was to be donated to science with the explicit instructions that she was not to be fingerprinted or otherwise identified. Her insistence that she never be officially recognized alive or dead is indeed curious. On October 26, an article appeared in the Woodbridge, New Jersey, *Times Tribune*. In part, it stated:

After her death, rumors surfaced that [Irene Bolam] was, in fact, Amelia Earhart, the famous aviatrix who disappeared on a flight between Lae, New Guinea, and Howland Island on 2 July 1937. Now, Irene Bolam's fingerprints are one of [New Jersey's] best kept secrets.

Irene Bolam's prints were denied to police agencies, the county prosecutor, Mrs. Bolam's doctor, state medical examiners, hospital authorities, and Mrs. Bolam's immediate family. Each person, in turn, had either found no standing to enter the case or had come up against a legal stone wall.

The death certificate was dated August 17, 1982. All of the spaces on the death certificate were filled out except for two that requested the names of the deceased's mother and father. Both sections were marked "Unknown."

A man who claimed to be Irene Bolam's son—Clarence Heller—expressed an interest in pursuing a solution to the Earhart-Bolam controversy but was denied. Heller's wife was quoted as saying that the officials at the medical school where Bolam's body had been sent had disguised the corpse "in some manner so that only one or two people in the school knew which . . . was hers." She also said that "the attorney for the school told her that a prior arrangement made with Mrs. Bolam precluded the release of her fingerprints."

In other words, not only did Bolam refuse to provide fingerprints while she was alive, she made arrangements to keep them a secret after her death. One cannot help but wonder why. According to author Reineck, an April 23, 1992, letter from Dr. Gordon J. McDonald of the University of Medicine and Dentistry of New Jersey stated that Irene Bolam's body was ultimately cremated and the ashes were buried in an unmarked grave. The letter also stated that the medical school had no information regarding "any next of kin of Irene Bolam."

Bolam's death certificate was signed by Dr. Ming Fong Hsu of Roosevelt Hospital in Edison, New Jersey. He listed Guy Bolam as the individual providing Irene's personal information. Guy Bolam, however, had passed away twelve years earlier in 1970.

The notation of "unknown" applied to the form requesting the names of Bolam's parents, as well as the statement that the medical school had no information relating to Bolam's next of kin, are difficult to comprehend. Surely, such information would not have been difficult to obtain. What seems to be apparent was that there was an orchestrated attempt at keeping relevant identity information regarding Irene Craigmile Bolam from being obtained. The obvious question is why was this done? Research into the life of Irene

Craigmile Bolam from 1945 until her passing in 1982 reveals nothing that would necessitate or even suggest this level of secrecy. Unless, of course, Mrs. Bolam was, in fact, Amelia Earhart.

There exists an impressive body of evidence that carries the strong suggestion, if not outright logic, that:

1. Amelia Earhart was involved in a covert government-endorsed and government-sponsored operation wherein the objective was to take photographs of real and potential Japanese military installations on one or more of the mandated islands in the Pacific Ocean. This information was kept from the American public.
2. Earhart friend and navigator Fred Noonan survived the alleged "crashed and sank" event originated and perpetrated by the United States government .
3. Earhart and Noonan were captured by the Japanese military and held prisoner, perhaps as long as eight years.
4. Earhart was liberated from a Japanese prison camp in China and repatriated to the United States under a new identity—Irene Craigmile.
5. There exists a litany of mysteries—solved and unsolved—revolving around the disappearance of Earhart, mysteries that add layer upon layer of suspicion and enigma related to government involvement and cover-up.
6. Earhart lived out the remainder of her life under a different identity—Irene Craigmile Bolam—and remained unknown to the world at large but well known to close friends and intimates.

Despite the abundance of evidence and the clear indication that Earhart was involved in a clandestine operation and resumed life under a new identity, there exist a number of traditionalists who cling to the government's position and who further deny any credibility in, and seek to discredit, the Amelia Earhart–Irene Craigmile Bolam association. In their effort to "prove" that Irene Craigmile Bolam was not Amelia Earhart, a handful of enthusiasts employing Internet sites—among them Ronald Bright, Mike Campbell, and Bill Prymak—have focused on a few select associations but ignore the entire body of evidence available. They have stated that "no hard evidence exists to support an Earhart survival theory." The truth is that such evidence—from a number of sources and at a variety of levels—is quite abundant. The aforementioned Earhart hobbyists, along with a few others, adhere to the U.S.

government position that the aviatrix crashed and sank near Howland Island. Their arguments, all of which add to the great theater of Earhart drama and theory, conveniently ignore the abundance of the related mysteries, circumstances, contradictions, confusions, and clear attempts at deception.

For example, while the Earhart = Bolam debunkers have focused on government-supplied information and traditional versions of the flight around the world and its aftermath to maintain a certain historical status quo, they have conveniently disregarded or overlooked the array of other mysteries surrounding the Earhart case, including: the Howland Island conundrum, the clandestine visits of Bernard Baruch and Admiral Westover with Earhart, the modifications of the Electra, including the installation of cameras, the Wilbur Rothar mystery, the tampering with the logs from the *Itasca*, the illogical and botched search for the Electra, the changes in the flight path, the government files on Earhart labeled top secret, the Mili Atoll landing, the false information released by the U.S. government related to weather during Earhart's disappearance, Earhart's role as a spy, the controversy involving Fred Noonan, the mystery letter sent to Jaluit, the government document that refers to Earhart's application for Japanese citizenship, the Tokyo Rose controversy, the Morgenthau memo, the discovery of the Electra at Aslito Airfield, the Forrestal mystery, the circumstances involving Forrestal's death, the Weihsien Prison Camp rescue, Irene Craigmile Bolam, Guy Bolam, Irene Bolam's refusal to be fingerprinted or otherwise identified, Irene Bolam's confusing death certificate, and more.

There exist several Amelia Earhart–related Internet sites that do little more than add to the confusion and do little to assist in resolving anything. An example of one is "The Controversial History of Amelia Earhart's Last Flight and Most Prominent Survival Account." The site lists as authors and contributors Randall Brink, Fred Goerner, Vincent Loomis, Joe Gervais, Donald Moyer Wilson, and Rollin Reineck. In a somewhat self-aggrandizing effort, the site is labeled by the authors as "academically objective."

Even a cursory examination of the site yields the notion that it would fail any test related to academic integrity, and there is certainly nothing objective about it.

One common argument that has been advanced by the vocal but small Earhart-is-not-Bolam group relates to the notion that the aviatrix was five feet, seven inches tall, in possession of a trim physique, and flat-chested, whereas Irene Craigmile Bolam was five feet, five inches tall, possessed of a "full physique," and had a plump, ample bosom and thus physically bore no resemblance to Earhart at all. Earhart enthusiast Ron Bright wrote, "I think it is pretty common knowledge that people who are skinny into their 40s generally remain skinny the rest of their lives." This absurd statement is contradicted by science, medical research and records, and everyday experience and observation.

Absent from this argument are factors relating to aging, health, stress, and logic. In 1965, when Irene Craigmile Bolam was identified by author Joe Gervais as possibly being Amelia Earhart, the aviatrix would have been sixty-eight years old. Data from physicians, medical specialists, chiropractors, health agencies, and other health-associated entities clearly show that as one ages, one's height and stature is easily and often reduced as a result of deterioration in the skeletal and cartilaginous structure, particularly in the area of the spine. Losing two inches in height during old age, say, from five feet, seven inches to five feet, five inches is not only a possibility, it is quite common.

Photographs and descriptions of Irene Craigmile Bolam portray her as a bit overweight, perhaps as much as forty pounds or more. Weight gain in the aged, like height reduction, is common and normal. The weight differences between Amelia Earhart and Irene Craigmile Bolam can be the result of aging, the ever-common hormonal changes related to such, diet, illness, stress, and sedentary lifestyle. It must also be pointed out that during her eight years of imprisonment, and given what has been learned about the terrible conditions at the Weihsien Prison camp in China, the notion of stress and physical trauma contributing to the state of her health and well-being cannot be discounted.

Another argument put forth by the traditionalists relates to the presumed notion that Earhart, if returning to the United States under an assumed identity, never made contact with her family, and they wonder in print how such a thing can come to pass. The doubters only assume that Earhart had no contact with family members. The possibility that she did exists.

Assuming for a moment that Earhart had been a prisoner of the Japanese for eight years, held under stressful conditions with inadequate nutrition and poor, if any, medical care, the woman who returned to the United States would be decidedly different in appearance, attitude, and mental state than the one who left on the around-the-world flight. Given that she quite possibly was involved in a failed government spy mission, given that she may have been associated with the infamous Tokyo Rose radio broadcasts, and given that evidence suggests that she may have actually colluded with the Japanese during her time there, it is little wonder that Amelia Earhart wanted nothing to do with that identity. She would become a marked woman. Furthermore, it can easily be concluded that her anonymity and assumed new identity was encouraged and abetted by the U.S. government and its leaders. If the truth had come out, a number of prominent political and military leaders would have suffered.

The only solution was to have the government maintain its oft-quoted "crash and sank" version of what happened on July 2, 1937, and facilitate the passage of the surviving Amelia Earhart into a new and different segment of society, hoping all the while that the deception, as well as those involved in perpetrating it, would never be found out.

· 43 ·

Analysis

History is a set of lies agreed upon.

—Napoleon Bonaparte

History would be a wonderful thing if only it were true.

—Leo Tolstoy

History doesn't repeat itself. Historians repeat each other.

—Oscar Wilde

*I*f Amelia Earhart and Fred Noonan crashed and sank near Howland Island in the Pacific Ocean during an around-the-world flight as the U.S. government insisted, then there would have been no reason to have all documents pertaining to such classified as top secret by the War Department. What could there possibly be in the files on the disappearance of a civilian aircraft that caused such a decision to be made? The obvious conclusion is that the sequence of events prior to, during, and following the disappearance of Earhart did not happen the way it was officially reported.

With the passage of three-quarters of a century, layer after layer of mystery and deception have been identified and peeled back bit by bit. In the process, the most reliable evidence that has surfaced and survived scrutiny points to the notion that the official line on what happened to Amelia Earhart and Fred Noonan is a lie, and furthermore, there is little to no evidence whatsoever to support the official version.

On the other hand, there exists an abundance of credible evidence to support the contention that Earhart survived, was taken prisoner, and was repatriated to the United States. The controversy surrounding the connection between Earhart and Irene Craigmile Bolam did little to dispel the ever-growing suspicion that the two women were the same and that Amelia Earhart, under a different identity, did indeed return from beyond the grave.

The question that naturally arises when considering the Amelia Earhart–Irene Bolam connection is: If people knew of Earhart's repatriation and her new life under an alias, and there were many who knew, how could it have been kept a secret for so long?

There are a couple of ways of looking at this conundrum. It is clear that a number of people were aware of Earhart's secret identity and that they kept it among themselves for the most part, being somewhat protective of her privacy. The truth is, Earhart's new identity was not as secret as some like to believe.

It must also be pointed out that there are several historic cases on record of people who have "died" or "disappeared" and returned under different identities and led relatively quiet and secretive lives. These individuals were visited and identified by their long-time companions but remained relatively unknown to the rest of the world.

There are several important examples of noted individuals living "beyond the grave." One of the most famous was the outlaw Billy the Kid. Alleged to have been shot and killed by Sheriff Pat Garrett in 1881, the Kid, whose real name was William Henry Roberts, survived and lived in hiding for most of the rest of his life under aliases. He died in 1950 in Texas. The evidence for his return and amazing life is documented in the book *Billy the Kid: Beyond the Grave* (Taylor Trade, 2005).

The results and subsequent reporting of the investigation into Roberts represented a dramatic and significant departure from the long-accepted, traditional history of the outlaw, but the evidence was there and is yet to be refuted. The traditional history, as it turned out, amounted to little more than so-called historians repeating what Sheriff Pat Garrett wrote in his now oft-discredited book, *The Authentic Life of Billy the Kid*. Once this was done, the historians simply repeated one another over the years. An examination of the hundreds of books and articles related to Billy the Kid reveals there is little in the way of original research presented in any of them and no investigation whatsoever.

Another famous outlaw, Butch Cassidy, was reputed to have perished in a shootout with the Bolivian army in 1908. The truth, however, is that the shootout never happened and was a concoction of a writer of fiction as well as the film industry and accepted as legitimate history by the public. In fact, Cassidy, whose real name was Robert Leroy Parker, returned to the United

States, where he lived out the remainder of his life, eventually passing away in Spokane, Washington, in 1937 (*Butch Cassidy: Beyond the Grave*, Taylor Trade, 2012).

John Wilkes Booth, the assassin of President Abraham Lincoln, lived under aliases for thirty-eight years following his escape from Ford's Theater in 1865. His story is detailed in *John Wilkes Booth: Beyond the Grave* (Taylor Trade, 2013).

The same pattern was followed in the studies and research related to Amelia Earhart: it is easier to repeat what others have written than it is to conduct intensive and meaningful investigation into the subject.

There are other examples, but these few point out that it lies well within the realm of possibility and probability that an individual can "die" or "disappear" and then return at a later date and live in relative anonymity for decades.

Monsignor James Francis Kelley's role in the Irene Craigmile Bolam controversy has been attacked and criticized by some who remain tethered to the U.S. government version of Earhart's fate. They are quick to point out that Kelley made up his role in repatriating the aviatrix and that in his later years had slipped mentally, perhaps suffered from dementia, and was prone to telling outrageous stories. To refer to one who holds an opposing point of view as a nut is a common tactic with those who disagree with their contentions. To demean a source of information is easy; to take the time and apply the energy necessary to study and understand the available information and place oneself in the position of offering intelligent critical thought requires some effort.

If Monsignor Kelley was clearly prone to the above-mentioned transgressions and was demented, he would not have been named president of Seton Hall College (now Seton Hall University). Nor would he have been part of a social circle that included the likes of Franklin D. Roosevelt, Harry S. Truman, J. Edgar Hoover, Charles Lindbergh, Cardinal Spellman, and more, a circle in which he was active and in which he thrived until his passing.

Mrs. Helen Barber was a friend of Monsignor Kelley and his neighbor on St. Croix Island. In 1981, when Kelley was seventy-eight years old, he and Barber were having lunch together when he related to her his role in rehabilitating Amelia Earhart. He was selected, he said, by his friend Cardinal Spellman because of his background in psychiatry and his Jungian-related studies. He told Barber that he boarded Earhart in his New Jersey estate and provided her with "spiritual, emotional, and psychological help." He confessed that he worked closely with U.S. government officials in selecting a new identity for Earhart. Kelley also related to Barber that Earhart was adamant about keeping her survival and return to the United States secret. The extant evidence supports Kelley's version of events.

Confirming Helen Barber's story was Donald DeKoster. Like Barber, DeKoster had been a neighbor and friend of Monsignor Kelley and had known him for well over a decade. DeKoster told interviewer and author Rollin C. Reineck that he and Kelley had discussed the Earhart-Bolam episode a number of times, that he, Kelley, assisted in her return to the United States, that Earhart refused to maintain her true identity, and that she feared being associated with the Tokyo Rose affair. Kelley related a number of details relative to his connection with church and U.S. government officials that left DeKoster with no doubt of Kelley's involvement and veracity. Kelley told DeKoster that Amelia Earhart and Irene Craigmile Bolam were one and the same person.

It may well be a fact that Monsignor Kelley suffered dementia during his later years, but well before he grew infirm his role in the repatriation of Amelia Earhart was known to a number of political, military, and church leaders. It was only Kelley's detractors who played the dementia card; those who knew the monsignor well never considered it an issue.

It is a truth that the families of both Amelia Earhart and Irene Craigmile Bolam have never fully cooperated in the resolution of the identity mystery. At one time, Earhart's sister, Muriel Morrissey, admitted she was "friends" with Irene Craigmile Bolam. There was little likelihood that Morrissey would have ever encountered Bolam during the normal courses of their lives. This leads to the supposition that the two sisters did indeed communicate during their lifetimes.

Over the years, the anti-Irene Craigmile Bolam = Amelia Earhart faction has been vocal in insisting that Earhart never returned to the United States, that she certainly perished in a crash in the Pacific Ocean. While insistent, however, they have provided no substantive evidence whatsoever for their position, only parroting the government line and maintaining the status quo.

Opponents of the Earhart = Bolam connection have stated that they have "proved" there is no relationship whatsoever. The truth is, they have proved nothing—they have only offered opinions related to one side of the controversy.

At one point during his investigation and research, Joe Gervais received a letter from Irene Craigmile Bolam. In the missive, she stated, in reference to people she named, "each knew us well as Amelia Earhart and Irene Craigmile." This is a telling statement.

Another statement made by Earhart's close friend Jackie Cochran is likewise revealing. At an event honoring heroic female pilots, Earhart's name was brought up. In response, Cochran said, "Amelia would never show her face here after what she did."

What, exactly, did Cochran know? Cochran was regarded by many as being Earhart's best friend. It was long rumored that Cochran, as well as a few other acquaintances, was aware of Earhart's repatriation and new identity.

In the end, the evidence in support of Amelia Earhart surviving her ill-fated around-the-world flight and living out her years until 1982 is far greater and more substantive than the evidence against it.

America's "first lady of the air" led an adventure-filled life and became a prominent worldwide personality and celebrity. She did not disappear during her planned flight around the world as reported but for the next eight years found herself in a troubled, conflicting, disastrous, and destructive environment and way of life. From this she was eventually rescued, but she was never the same—in name, personality, or intentions, never returned to her previous status as one of the world's most admired women. But the preponderance of evidence suggests that she *did* return but lived out her life in relative obscurity and anonymity for thirty-seven years.

Who can fully appreciate how her life had changed as a result of her experiences, her imprisonment, her clandestine repatriation? Who can know about the nightmares she must have endured and the adjustments that had to be made in order for her to return to some semblance of a normal life? There is so much to learn, so much more information about this amazing woman that has yet to come to light. The search continues.

Selected Bibliography

Backus, Jean L. *Letters from Amelia*. Boston: Beacon, 1982.

Blau, Melinda. *Whatever Happened to Amelia?* New York: Contemporary Perspectives, 1977.

Bowman, David K. *Legerdemain*. Shaw, CA: Saga, 2007.

Brennan, T. C. "Buddy." *Witness to the Execution*. Frederick, CO: Renaissance House, 1988.

Briand, Paul. *Daughter of the Sky*. New York: Pyramid, 1967.

Butler, Susan. *East to the Dawn: The Life of Amelia Earhart*. Reading, MA: Addison-Wesley, 1997.

Campbell, Mike. *Amelia Earhart: The Truth at Last*. Camp Hill, PA: Sunbury, 2012.

———. *With Our Own Eyes*. With Thomas Devine. Lancaster, OH: Lucky, 2002.

Carrington, George Carson. *Amelia Earhart: What Really Happened at Howland Island*. Vancouver, BC: ITMB, 1989.

Devine, Thomas, and Richard Daley. *Eyewitness: The Amelia Earhart Incident*. Frederick, CO: Renaissance House, 1987.

Earhart, Amelia. *Last Flight*. New York: Harcourt, Brace, 1937.

———. *20 Hrs. 40 Min.: Our Flight in the Friendship*. New York: Putnam, 1928.

Garst, Doris Shannon. *Amelia Earhart*. New York: J. Messner, 1947.

Goerner, Fred. *The Search for Amelia Earhart*. New York: Doubleday, 1966.

Hagen, Barbara Shook. *Amelia's Flying Machine*. Garden City, NY: Doubleday, 1966.

Kaya, Y., and K. Kobayashi. "A Basic Study on Human Faces Recognition." In *Frontiers of Pattern Recognition*, edited by S. Watanabe, 265–289. New York: Academic, 1972.

Kennedy, Arthur. *High Times: Keep 'Em Flying*. With Jo Ann Ridley. Santa Barbara, CA: Fithin, 1992.

Klaas, Joe. *Amelia Earhart Lives*. New York: McGraw-Hill, 1970.

Knaggs, Oliver. *Amelia Earhart: Her Last Flight*. Cape Town, South Africa: Howard Timmons, 1983.

Long, Elgen M., and Marie K. Long. *Amelia Earhart: The Mystery Solved*. New York: Simon and Schuster, 1999.

Loomis, Vincent. *Amelia Earhart: The Final Story*. With Jeffrey L. Ethell. New York: Random House, 1985.

Mann, Peggy. *Amelia Earhart*. New York: Coward-McCann, 1970.

Morrissey, Muriel Earhart, and Carol L. Osborne. *Amelia, My Courageous Sister*. Santa Clara, CA: Osborne, 1987.

———. *Courage Is the Price: The Biography of Amelia Earhart*. Wichita, KS: McCormick-Armstrong, 1963.

Myers, Robert H. *Stand by to Die*. Pacific Grove, CA: Lighthouse Writer's Guild, 1985.

O'Connor, Richard. *Winged Legend*. New York: Putnam, 1970.

Pellegreno, Ann Holtgren. *World Flight: The Earhart Trail*. Ames: Iowa State University Press, 1971.

Putnam, George Palmer. *Soaring Wings*. New York: Harcourt, Brace, 1939.

Reineck, Rollin C. *Amelia Earhart Survived*. Orange, CA: Paragon Agency, 2003.

Tannous, Peter. *The Earhart Mission*. New York: Simon and Schuster, 1978.

Thayer, James Stewart. *The Earhart Betrayal*. New York: Putnam, 1980.

Wilson, Donald Moyer. *Amelia Earhart: Lost Legend*. Webster, NY: Enigma, 1994.

About the Author

W.C. Jameson is the award-winning author of more than ninety books. He lives and writes in Texas.